It Don't Get Any Better Than This

It Don't Get Any Better Than This

Stories from a Small-Town Church

David A. Shirey

"Folk Village" by Karla Gerard, Artist, www.karlagerard.com

Book design by Adam Thomas.

ISBN: 979-8-9883293-0-5 (paperback)
ISBN: 979-8-9883293-1-2 (e-book)

This book is memoir. It reflects the author's recollections of experiences forty years ago. Though all the incidents are real, the author, a storyteller at heart, has told them in a way that evokes the feeling and meaning of what took place. Embellishments? Yes. Fabrications? No. The dialogue comes from the author's recollections and journals. It does not represent word-for-word transcripts, though some is verbatim. It does convey the character and personality of the speakers. All persons within are actual individuals; there are no composite or fictional characters. No effort has been made whatsoever to disguise the author's abiding appreciation and affection for the people whose stories are chronicled in these pages.

Printed in the United States of America.

First edition 2013
Polar Star Press
Disciples of Christ Historical Society
Nashville, TN

Second Edition 2023
David A. Shirey
3085 Montavesta Rd.
Lexington, KY 40502

www.davidashirey.com

For Dr. Herman A. Norton

Contents

Introduction

I thank my God in all my remembrance of you, always in every prayer of mine for you all making my prayer with joy, thankful for your partnership in the gospel from the first day until now. And I am sure that he who began a good work in you will bring it to completion at the day of Jesus Christ."

–Philippians 1:3-6, RSV

My Philippi was in Tennessee. Paul's first church on European soil was in Philippi. The first church I served was in Carthage, Tennessee. For two and a half years while in seminary, I pastored Carthage Christian Church (Disciples of Christ), average worship attendance of 20. Every Sunday morning I'd drive sixty miles from Nashville to Carthage. I'd cross the bridge over the Cumberland River, pass the Smith County Courthouse on the left, eye the Mom and Pop stores lining the square on the right, go another block and pull into the last diagonal parking place in front of the modest red brick building, est. 1875.

My wife and I began dating during my tenure there. When eighty-something-year-old Miss Margaret wrecked her car and injured one of her keyboard-playing hands, twenty-something Jennie subbed for her. Jennie got ten dollars a week. I got seventy-five. For both of us, it was a labor of love among God's beloved: Mr. Bill and Billie Ruth, Kenneth and Frances Sue, Miss Ella, 100-year-old Miz McGinness, forgetful Aunt Hazel, snowbirds Harry and Ova, mandolin-playing Chet Paris and his wife Edna, Polly and her to-die-for chicken and dumplings, her son Mike, her daughter Wanda and her boys Travis and Lyle, the Robinsons (David, Ramona, Amanda, and Tyler), the Dixons, eighteen-wheeler John Collette, his wife, Lib (seamstress of my wife's wedding dress), and their daughter Leann.

Their names are as special as any of the names in the Bible. We skip over the biblical lists of names to get to the good stuff because we don't know Jaha'ziel from Jekame'am. God does, though. God knows the names of the faithful, including the two dozen members of Carthage Christian Church circa 1985. They are each beloved of God.

They are beloved in my eyes, too. How could they not be? They sat through my first attempts at preaching. They took turns having me over for Sunday dinner— fried chicken, collard greens, cornbread, and apple pie. When Miss Ella died, I did my first funeral. When Leann and Randy got married, I did my first wedding. When Amanda, Tyler, and Lyle showed up by 10:00 a.m. or so on Sunday, Jennie and I taught our first Sunday school classes. She taught the younger elementary-aged class: Amanda and Lyle. I taught the older elementary division: Travis. At the ripe old age of twenty-two, they called me to be their pastor. At age twenty-five, I knelt at the chancel steps and faced the communion table as they laid hands on and ordained me.

The church is no more and neither are many of them. The last worship service was held on October 22, 1995. The building itself burned to the ground on April 14, 2004. A manila envelope arrived in the mail at our Phoenix home bearing the return address of Kenneth Robinson postmarked Carthage, TN. I opened the envelope, pulled out a folded copy of *The Carthage Courier* ("Tennessee's Oldest Newspaper Proudly Serving Smith County Since 1807"), and read the banner headline: "Fire, Destruction, Tragedy." Beneath it was a photo of the red brick building on Main, in the shelter of whose wings I was nurtured, engulfed in flames, smoke billowing through the roof. Additional headlines on the front page read: "Three Firemen Injured as Historical Church Destroyed" (Fire Chief Ed Stallings would later die of his injuries), "Thursday Blaze Not an Ordinary Fire," and "Church Stood for Well Over a Century."

Photographs accompanying the building's obituary documented the destruction. One showed a lone, weary fireman, hose limply resting on his shoulder, looking out over the smoldering rubble toward what was the entrance, front doors gone. Every week I entered those front doors I was welcomed by the mellifluous baritone drawl of Elder Alexander Campbell Read, Jr. (affectionately known as "Mr. Bill") intoning from the chancel steps within, "David Shirey, come into this house!" That weekly liturgical welcome cultivated a miracle of sorts: a twenty-two-year-old Yankee whose house and kin were several hundred miles and another culture away was made to feel at home and among family in a small Southern town.

Now the church was no more. I wrote a shorthand requiem in my journal that day, then folded up the newspaper clipping and filed it away in the closet with other Carthage memorabilia.

Four years passed. I arrived home one afternoon and checked the answering machine. The caller ID showed a call from the 615 area code: Nashville. Jennie saw the name of the caller — Glover, Randy — and asked, "Who's Randy Glover?"

I said, "Randy Glover married Leann Collette, John and Lib Collette's daughter from Carthage. Theirs was the first wedding I ever did."

I called Leann. She said she googled my name and called me because her eldest daughter was getting married and she wanted the minister who was going to officiate at her daughter's wedding to include something I had included in her and Randy's wedding 25 years ago. She caught me up on everybody. I told her she had made my day.

She said, "I just want you to know your first wedding took."

I told her I wanted her to know that my first church took, too — took me in, grew me up, and sent me forth into ministry before receiving yet another student pastor with open arms.

Their stories took, too. A quarter-century after I got up from my knees duly ordained by their laying on of hands, their stories remain. I live now in Phoenix, the namesake of the mythical risen-from-the-ashes bird, where I was called nearly a decade ago to start a new church from scratch. As I watch our new building go up, I'm mindful of the one that burned down and how the stories of a few dozen people of a church that lived to be a hundred have risen from the ashes.

They deserve retelling to remind us how a great God persists in choosing to be incarnate in small places among modest people — in mangers among shepherds and such.

Paul wrote to the Philippians, "I thank my God in all my remembrance of you, always in every prayer of mine for you all making my prayer with joy, thankful for your partnership in the gospel from the first day until now. And I am sure that he who began a good work in you will bring it to completion at the day of Jesus Christ."

Philippi was Paul's Carthage.

A Discordant Doxology

My pastorate at Carthage began off-key. Literally. The church had two instruments, a piano and a Wurlitzer organ that somebody probably donated to the church to get rid of it. I don't know that I ever heard it played and it's probably just as well.

I remember when the organ in our church in North Carolina got sick. It made a high-decibel groan that scared a guest organist who was practicing for an upcoming wedding. As soon as she gathered her wits about her she called and told us, "Your organ needs help," a fact Jennie and I confirmed upon turning it on and having the bejeebers scared out of us, too.

Jennie called an organ repair person, though given the hideous sound it was making an exorcist might have been in order. A guy came from somewhere in Virginia. After hearing the hideous groan, he confirmed, "Your organ needs help," and then spent several hours surgically removing and replacing various and sundry microchips before handing us a bill that evoked a high-decibel groan from our Financial Secretary.

While it was being repaired and we were wondering "What will we do without an organ?" I recalled the organ-related travail I encountered on my second Sunday at Carthage.

After Mr. Bill had greeted me with, "David Shirey, come into this house!," he told me eighty-some-year-old Margaret Westmoreland had had a serious automobile accident, that she would be out of commission for several months, that they could find no replacement for her, and that I would be leading the hymn-singing *a cappella* for the foreseeable future.

Not good. Of the twenty or so who regularly worshipped, maybe half of them sang ... sort of. Kenneth said he couldn't sing. John said he just plain wouldn't sing. Mike said if he did sing, we'd ask him not to. That left us with maybe a dozen "singers," folks who agreed to cast caution to the wind and make a joyful noise unto the Lord, regardless of the key the noise came out in.

We had a repertoire of about eight songs including "Holy, Holy, Holy," "Amazing Grace," "We're Marching to Zion," and "Revive Us Again." God knows we needed reviving, given the sound we made. One Sunday, I got us off on the wrong key and wrong beat on "Come, Thou Fount of Every Blessing." We went downhill from there until midway through the second verse Billie Ruth Read, who was standing in the front row, made a throat-slitting gesture with her right hand while imploring me, "Stop us, David! Stop us!"

I did. I stopped us after the second verse. "You may be seated," I said, to which Billie Ruth whispered, "Thank you!"

Margaret returned after months of rehabilitation. Bless her heart, she wanted to try playing the piano again. "Try" was her word. She had broken three of the fingers on her right hand during the accident and they had healed crooked. She told me that even though she couldn't play some of the chords quite right, she "thought she'd give it a try."

She did. She tried. She did fairly well on "All Hail the Power of Jesus' Name." "What a Friend We Have in Jesus" came off all right, too, but when we got to the Doxology her crooked fingers met their match. The opening bars evoked a collective wince. Twenty faces grimaced as we began to sing "Praise God from whom all blessings flow" to the contorted chords.

Billie Ruth didn't even have to tell us to stop. We just did. And after a few more broken bars of music, Margaret stopped, too.

What happened next I'll never forget. Eighty-some-year-old born and bred southern lady Margaret Westmoreland uttered an expletive. It was a rather tame one, but an unaccompanied, *a cappella* expletive nonetheless. Everybody heard it. Then without batting an eye, she drew a bead on me from the piano bench, pointed her crooked index finger my way, and barked, "Let's start again!"

Yes, Ma'am.

So, we started again. Margaret replayed the opening bars. This time they came out fine. Margaret smiled. Billie Ruth, standing in the front row, smiled, too, while shaking her head from side to side. As a matter of fact, we all smiled and sang along with more gusto than usual. In fact, Margaret's expletive, glare, and crooked finger point startled Kenneth, John, and Mike to the point that even they sang.

The maimed in hand and the lame of voice, we all stood together and sang "Praise God from whom all blessings flow."

Music Lessons

I had no business leading singing during Margaret's absence. Musical ability did not run in the family. Neither of my parents played an instrument. No one in my family sang.

When I aspired to join the Lincoln Elementary School band, my dad bought a tarnished trumpet at an auction. I tried to play it, but blow as I may, all I could produce were squeals and squawks, so I sat out the concerts, a decision neither the band teacher nor my parents challenged. When I packed the instrument back in its case, nobody contested that decision, either.

If my mouth couldn't produce music, maybe my hands could. In junior high, I saved money from my newspaper route and bought a cheap guitar. I took lessons at Danny Sapino's music store downtown with the aspiration of playing Paul Simon's "Homeward Bound." I practiced diligently, but my fingers produced no better music than my lips. Midway through a lesson, my instructor asked, "Do you hear how out of tune this is?"

I shook my head no, he winced, and I decided my guitar-playing days were over. Neither he nor my parents objected.

No quitter, I bought drumsticks and a practice pad. I took lessons two doors down from where I had taken guitar, but the change of scenery and instrument did not yield better results. I had no rhythm.

I bought a harmonica and aspired to play the lead-in to Neil Young's "Heart of Gold." Do I even need to go there?

In the fall of 1977, as a freshman at Indiana University, I looked for a church close to campus. First Christian Church (Disciples of Christ) was a bus ride and a five-block walk from my dormitory.

Why I did what I did next, I do not know. I went to the church during office hours, introduced myself to the secretary, and told her I wanted to join the choir. I shake my head and wonder, what was I thinking? He who had struck out on four instruments and never sang a note was presenting himself as a wannabe choir member. Little did I know it, but the secretary was the wife of the Director of the Singing Hoosiers, Indiana University's student Concert Choir.

"What part do you sing?" she asked.

"I'll sing any part or I'll sing all of it," I answered. "Whatever you need."

"I mean which *part* do you sing: soprano, alto, tenor, or bass?"

"I'll sing any of them. Whatever you need."

As I said, I knew *nothing*. She told me rehearsals were on Thursday evenings at 7 p.m. and I was welcome to join.

When I walked into the rehearsal room, I took a seat in the first open chair I spotted, which happened to be in the front row of the soprano section. Soon after, two men, elderly from my seventeen-year-old point of view, stood in front of me with their hands extended, introducing themselves. Harry Blewett and Bob Bartlett welcomed me and invited me to sit with them ... in the bass section. There began my four-year tutorial in choral singing.

I was handed a folder with the upcoming Sundays' anthems. I had entered a strange, new world. The black dots on the page, some filled in and others blank inside, the sets of parallel lines on which the notes were suspended, the words staggered in between—I was looking at hieroglyphics. When the Director cued the accompanist and everyone sang, I sat mute. Clueless.

Harry and Bob commenced their work. Harry whispered, "Follow my finger," and I tracked the notes as he led me. Bob leaned in and sang toward one ear and Harry did the same for the other, providing me a stereo soundtrack enabling me to link the pitch of their voices with the pointed-out notes.

Finally conscious of my ignorance and near tone deafness, I sang softly those first months. Better not to be heard than to sing out, be offbeat and off-pitch, and blow the cover of my incompetence. To paraphrase Lincoln, "Better to remain silent and be thought a fool than to *sing* and remove all doubt."

The Men's Chorus sang at the 8:30 a.m. service, after which Harry and Bob insisted on taking me across the street to Ladyman's Café for breakfast. It was always their treat. When at the end of my sophomore year I told them I had changed my major from Pre-Med to Religious Studies, our breakfast conversations turned to matters of faith and belief. Meanwhile, I continued to sit between them twice a week, learning to sing from their patient example.

On my last Sunday, May of 1981, they walked me out after worship was over and, extending their hands, wished me well. I remember both of their eyes glistening as I ignored their outstretched hands and reached out to give them each a hug. That was the last time I would see either of them.

Eighteen months later, emboldened by their lessons and with no one else to turn to, I stepped up and sang out with the cacophonous Carthage choir.

The Carthage Keyboard Controversy

It's a wonder Margaret even had a piano to play when she returned. I didn't know it at the time, but that instrument had been the source of a disharmony of much greater magnitude than our discordant Doxology and my off-pitch singing.

After the congregation declined in numbers to single digits in the early nineties, the faithful remnant sold the building to a Church of Christ congregation. With the money they received, they established a need-based scholarship fund for Smith County high school students desiring to go to college. Meanwhile, the building that for over a century was home to Carthage Christian Church sported a wooden sign above the front doors that read Main Street Church of Christ.

The reporter who covered the blaze for *The Carthage Courier* wrote, "With apologies to the Main Street Church of Christ congregation, I did not know there were two churches located on Main Street with such similar names," a reference to the Carthage Church of Christ located just down the street. He didn't know the relationship (or lack thereof) between the two Churches of Christ located just blocks apart nor do I, but I did hear the story of when a group of people left the Carthage Christian Church decades ago to take up residence down the street as the Carthage Church of Christ. The rift was provoked by a piano.

In the early forties, the Carthage Church split in two over the actions of a visiting evangelist at the annual revival. The Baptist and Methodist ministers in town were frequent attendees of the Christian Church's revivals back then and were often invited to participate. In 1943, however, the visiting evangelist, with the newly called pastor's backing, flatly refused to include the neighboring ministers. When asked why, he answered, "I will not call on sectarian preachers to lead in prayer at a Christian worship service." As he explained it, the Methodist preacher had never been immersed and the Baptist preacher wrapped himself in the "sectarian" title of Baptist as opposed to the "scripturally ordained" one of Christian. Bottom line: no unimmersed, sectarian ministers would be invited to participate in the revival. Take it or leave it.

The disagreement led to division; one church became two. Those who supported the views espoused by the visiting evangelist and minister became the Carthage Church of Christ. Those who urged the inclusion of neighboring pastors became the Carthage Christian Church (Disciples of Christ).

Soon after the split, the Christian Church congregation purchased a piano for the sanctuary. Previous to that time, the congregation had sung all their music *a cappella* because the more conservative members of the church roundly denounced "sectarians'" use of instrumental music in worship, claiming the New Testament made no mention of pianos and such and thus implicitly prohibiting them. Word of the Disciples' purchase of a piano only served to heighten the denunciations from the disaffected members. An article was published in the regional Church of Christ newsletter lambasting the "liberal" faction of the church for their admittance of "sectarians" to pray and for their purchase of a piano. The article was entitled "The Church at Carthage, TN, Goes Digressive." The rift was sealed.

During that painful period, a young woman whose family had left the church approached Brother Read, the long-time elder of the Disciples congregation, with a question. Brother Read was Alexander Campbell Read, Senior, father of "David Shirey, come into this house!" Elder Alexander Campbell Read, Junior. The woman was engaged to be married and wanted to know if it would be possible for her to be married in the sanctuary. Brother Read, in the gentle way which was reportedly his, nodded his head slowly, and in his deep, slow drawl, said, "Of course, daughter. The Lord's House is always open to you."

Whereupon she asked a second question, "Could the piano be played at my wedding?"

"Of course, daughter," the beloved Elder responded, "but the piano we purchased is on order and hasn't arrived yet so I'll have some of the men from the church move the piano from our house to the sanctuary in time for your wedding."

The girl's wedding was held in the Carthage Christian Church. Members of the Carthage Church of Christ and Carthage Christian Church sat side-by-side in the pews witnessing the vows. Piano music was added to the ceremony.

After the wedding, the bride, the groom, her family, and the Church of Christ folks returned to the building down the street where they continued worshiping God apart from liberal sectarians and unaided by non-scriptural things such as pianos.

Records indicate that three years later, in 1946, a certain Margaret Ligon Westmoreland became the pianist at Carthage Christian Church. She would play there throughout the next half century, broken fingers and all, until she died in 1994.

Tattoos on the Soul

Regardless of how poorly we sang, my years at Carthage instilled within me an appreciation for the power of sacred music. At a minister's retreat, Dr. Rick Harrison urged us to "sing some of the old songs" in worship from time to time. "The power of the old gospel hymns," he said, "lies in their ability to take us back to times and places gone by." He's right.

Mr. Bill used to ask, "David Shirey, when are we going to sing 'The Church in the Wildwood?'" Every once in a while we'd sing it. When we did, I could see Mr. Bill wasn't with us. He had taken leave of the premises. He was somewhere else. I asked him, "What is it with 'The Church in the Wildwood?'" He said, "My daddy had a deep bass voice and whenever we sing 'The Church in the Wildwood' I can hear his voice singing the refrain 'O come, come, come, come.'" Music took him there.

My mother died six years ago, but I can still hear her say, "We don't sing 'The Old Rugged Cross' enough at our church. When I was a little girl, your grandmother used to take me and your Aunt Bebe and walk us down Tod Avenue to Cherry Street to Emmanuel Lutheran Church. We sang the 'Old Rugged Cross' all the time." I noticed when we did sing "The Old Rugged Cross" that my mother would have a faraway look in her eyes. She was back in 1942, a six-year-old girl in pigtails sitting next to her mother and sister in Warren, Ohio.

Music can get deep down inside us. Neuroscientists tell us we have two hemispheres in our brain – the left is our logical hemisphere (where language resides) and the right is our creative hemisphere (where music resides). Music taps into the power of the right hemisphere of our brains and then right into our hearts and souls. It burrows deep down into the marrow, abiding with us even when we've forgotten much else.

Sarah S. Miller told of visiting her mother-in-law over the Christmas holidays in a facility where she was living after a debilitating stroke that claimed her faculties, including her memory. Her visit was marked by carolers:

They sang Christmas carols from an old book of hymns, and when they came to "Silent Night" I could hardly believe my ears. Mom was singing too. Her voice was soft, but she was on key and she knew the words. Everybody was stunned, but they kept on singing. They smiled at her and she nodded. They sang other carols and then went on to some of Mom's favorite hymns— "Amazing Grace," "What a Friend We Have in Jesus," "Holy, Holy, Holy." She sang them all.

It was a moment of incredible warmth and joy, blessing and almost magical beauty. Even when she couldn't recognize the faces of her own children, even when she seemed incapable of laughter or tears, the songs of faith were still alive. Deep within her spirit, well below the frost line of illness and loss, the hymns survived. ("Below the Frost Line, Hymns of Faith," *The Christian Century*, December 12, 1990.)

Jack Boyd, who taught church music and music history at Abilene Christian University, likened the capacity of music to leave such an indelible mark on the memory as "a tattoo on the subconscious."

One Christmas Eve twenty-five years ago, I had come home from the 11 o'clock Candlelight Communion Service, taken off my suit and tie, and was getting ready for bed when the phone rang. It was Joan, a woman in my church who was a volunteer chaplain at the hospital. She had drawn the short straw to be on call Christmas Eve. A woman keeping vigil with her comatose elderly mother asked for a chaplain.

"David," she said, "I don't know what to say. Would you go with me?"

We met at the nursing station and pondered what we would do. When we decided on our plan, we walked down to the room. A middle-aged woman was sitting next to her aged mother's bed, gently stroking her hand.

"She's not responding," she said. "The doctors say it's only a matter of time. Mother may not know you're here, but I do. Thank you for coming."

Then Joan and I did what we discerned we would do. We knelt at the woman's bedside and sang softly, "Silent night, holy night, all is calm, all is bright / Round yon virgin Mother and Child / Holy infant so tender and mild."

As we sang, the woman began to move her lips to form the words we were singing. No sound came out, but the shape of the words did: "Sleep in heavenly peace / Sleep in heavenly peace."

At that, she took her last breaths with her daughter at her side and slept in heavenly peace. “Deep within her spirit, well below the frost line of illness and loss, the hymns survived.” Tattoos on the soul.

Mr. Bill wanted to sing “The Church in the Wildwood.” My mother pestered her pastor for “The Old Rugged Cross.” For me, a few bars of “We’re Marching to Zion” or “Revive Us Again,” not to mention a discordant Doxology, takes me back to Carthage.

We sound as bad as ever. It’s beautiful.

Ten Bucks and a Free Ride

When I began at Carthage I knew nothing of the keyboard controversy. Neither did I know when Margaret drew that bead on me and barked from the piano bench, "Let's start again!" that my future wife would play the same instrument.

After Margaret's foot got stuck on the accelerator while trying to back out of the driveway, sending her car hurtling in reverse into a sprawling, centuries-old live oak tree, her into the hospital, and us out of a keyboard player, Billie Ruth Read came to me with a proposition.

"David," she said, "We need a pianist."

She was right. By then it was obvious that I was not cut out to be an *a cappella* song leader. What's more, our repertoire of the half dozen songs to which we could (sort of) carry the tune was getting old. Our "We're Marching to Zion" was dragging. Our "Bringing in the Sheaves" was coming up empty. "Amazing Grace" had become routine. We needed a "Blessed Assurance" that some enlivening accompaniment was on the way.

Billie Ruth directed me to go back to Nashville, post a

"Help Wanted" ad in the vicinity of Vanderbilt, and select from among the applicants who would best fill the position. When I inquired about salary she said she and Mr. Bill had talked it over and were willing to pay ten dollars a week.

I thought to myself — an hour's drive over, an hour of worship, and an hour's drive back to Nashville for ten bucks? And I was to decide for myself among all the applicants? All?

I kept my skepticism to myself. I smiled and told Billie Ruth I'd advertise the position. I would even be willing to match her and Mr. Bill's munificence with an offer of my own. The lucky person selected from our teeming pool of applicants would be offered free round-trip travel to and from Carthage in the passenger seat of my 1978 Chrysler LeBaron. Billie Ruth said she thought that would be wonderful. I smiled again.

There were no takers. I figured as much. Who in their right mind would make a one hundred twenty-mile commute to play a Wurlitzer Funmaker or its piano partner sidekick for a congregation of a baker's dozen, let alone having to listen week in and week out to a greenhorn preacher? We carried on *a cappella* for the next several months until Margaret finally returned.

A few months after Margaret was back, I met a woman at Vanderbilt. After we dated several times and I got my nerve up, I told her I was serving a little church out in Carthage and would she like to go with me some Sunday morning? Talk about a slick come-on: "Hey baby, wanna hear me preach?"

She said yes.

When I found out in time that she played piano and asked if she would consider playing at Carthage some Sunday, she said she would. Margaret welcomed her with open arms (one of which was still rehabbing from the accident). She played one Sunday. Then another. On one of our Sunday morning drive dates, she mentioned she remembered seeing a piece of paper several months earlier advertising the need for a pianist at a small church and had almost followed up on it out of curiosity before forgetting about it altogether.

"Little did I know," she said.

Little did either of us know. Jennie Taylor ended up making the round trip to Carthage with me in the LeBaron Sunday in and Sunday out for a year and a half until we got married. She received ten dollars a week for her piano playing and from Lib Collette, church member and seamstress, she received the handmade wedding dress she wore on our wedding day.

The Proposal

The courtship that culminated in my proposing marriage to Jennie and prompted Lib Collette to make her wedding dress involved a Confederate statue.

The week after Christmas in 1983, I flew from Indianapolis, IN, to Richmond, VA, with a ring in my pocket, prepared to propose to Jennie. I missed my flight, had to wait for another connection, and arrived in Richmond at 11:00 p.m.

My initial plan was to suggest to Jennie on the forty-minute drive from Richmond to the village of Amelia where her parents lived in their retirement that we stop at the courthouse square and take a walk before going to the house so I could stretch a bit. I would then pop the question on bended knee in front of the courthouse where her grandfather had served as an esteemed attorney and judge. Given my missed flight, we did not pull into Amelia until after midnight, but I decided to press on with my plan nonetheless.

"How about a walk before we go to the house?" I asked.

"At a quarter after twelve? Are you kidding me?"

"No," I said, pretending to be nonchalant and with a ring burning a hole in my pocket. "I've been sitting in an airport for six hours and on a plane for another hour and a half. I want to stretch and get some fresh air."

She pulled into one of the diagonal parking places on the courthouse square. Needless to say, we had the place to ourselves.

We made a lap around the courthouse square and when we got back toward the car, I steered us toward the backside of the Confederate War Dead Memorial, knelt, and asked her to marry me.

She said, "Yes."

I told her family the next morning that I proposed at the rear end of the memorial for fear that the ghost of a Confederate soldier, hearing a Yankee stealing away a daughter of the South, would have filled my backside with gunpowder. So, I snuck behind– out of sight, out of mind– and did my bidding.

Even then, I knew Confederate statues evoke all kinds of emotions, many of them volatile and, if pressed, capable of violence.

Carthage had its own monuments to the Confederacy. The Smith County Courthouse, one block south of the church, was built at the end of Reconstruction in 1875. Northwest of the square is the City Cemetery, where confederate veterans are buried. A United Daughters of the Confederacy monument stands on the courthouse grounds. To the east of the square was the town's Reconstruction-era African American neighborhood, marked by historic African-American congregations and what was called Carthage Colored High School.

On Sundays when I arrived early, I took a walk down

Main Street with the manuscript of my sermon in hand and committed it to memory as I circled the courthouse square and Carthage's antebellum, Reconstruction, and Jim Crow history.

Adjacent to the square is Braden Chapel United Methodist Church, a historic African American congregation. The Braden Chapel congregation made and sold carryout dinners every first Sunday of the month as a fundraiser for their ministries. On one of my first Sundays, Mr. Bill accompanied me to Braden Chapel.

"David Shirey," he said, "I want to introduce you to two of the finest people you'll ever meet, Mr. Roy Carter and his wife, Mrs. Robbie Key Carter. Not only are they among God's finest human beings, but I also count them as friends. What's more, Mrs. Carter makes the best fried pies in Smith County. I've ordered some to take home with us along with our Sunday dinners. My, my, have you got something to look forward to!"

At Mr. Bill's introduction, I met Mr. Roy and Ms. Robbie Key ("This is David Shirey, our pastor from Vanderbilt. He's a fine young man"). They welcomed me into their friendship. Thereafter, every first Sunday, I showed up at Braden Chapel at 12:15 p.m. with a check from Mr. Bill for three Sunday dinners, fried pies, and occasionally, a chocolate pie, another of Mrs. Carter's specialties.

After exchanging pleasantries with Mr. Roy and Ms. Robbie Key and being introduced by them to other members of their congregation ("This is Brother David Shirey, pastor at the Christian Church. He's a fine young man"), Roy would ask me what I preached on. As the meals and pies were being prepared, I'd give him a précis of my sermon. When laden with the goods, I'd thank the Carters and the cooks and head to Mr. Bill and Billie Ruth's for some of the best food I ever put in my mouth. Mr. Bill, a napkin tucked into his collar, would Ooh and Aah until he'd say, "Now for those fruit pies!" at which time Billie Ruth would feign exasperation at her beloved, saying, "Bill Read, you need one of Robbie Key's pies like you need a hole in the head." Whereupon Mr. Bill would chuckle, take a bite of that cinnamon and sugar-covered pastry, and break out in more Oohs and Aahs.

Recently, I looked through photographs from my ordination at Carthage. As I thumbed through them, I named aloud the people who made the trek to Smith County that day from points north, south, east, and west. Many are gone now. Many of the signatures on my ordination certificate are faded with time. I came to a photo I had not remembered: the Carters. They are side-by-side with Polly Alcorn in a pew. Mr. Roy is dressed to the nines in a dark suit and tie. Ms. Robbie Key wears a broad-rimmed bonnet with a white ribbon and a string of pearls around her neck. In another photo, Mr. Roy and I stand side-by-side, his right arm around my waist.

I went to my computer, typed "Roy Carter," "Braden Chapel" and "Carthage, TN" into the search engine, and pressed enter. It turned up an obituary that read:

Mrs. Robbie Key Garrett Carter entered into eternal rest and transferred to her heavenly home at 9:21 p.m. Thursday evening November 7, 2019. In Carthage in 1949, she was united in marriage to Stonewall Community native, the late Willie Roy Carter who transitioned to his heavenly home on July 18, 1994, at the age of 69. Her beloved husband and the father of their five children was a Smith County educator, occupational therapist at the Alvin C. York Medical Center in Murfreesboro, and also a longtime employee of the Citizens Bank in Carthage. Mrs. Carter professed her faith in Christ at a young age and became a faithful and dedicated member of the Braden United Methodist Church on the Square in Carthage. Her church family always looked forward to the fried fruit pies and chocolate pies she provided at church functions and which she often delivered with a warm smile to her friends in the Carthage Community.

Looking back over forty years, I recognize how ignorant I was of the injustice, bigotry, racism, and discrimination memorialized in brick and stone that I so casually walked around on those Sunday mornings at the Courthouse Square. Nor did I comprehend the menace aimed at such as the Carters in Jim Crow years by those who dedicated the monument behind which I knelt to propose nearly forty years ago.

In recent years, Jennie has gathered Black and white women to talk openly about racism. Thanks to the intrepid Black women who are part of the group, my wife, a daughter of Virginia, can see with new eyes what Faulkner called "the past that is not even past." Under their patient tutelage, she is being schooled in new ways of being white. In former Kentucky Poet Laureate Frank X. Walker's clarion words, she proposes to "unlearn fear and hate."

That's my proposal, too, God help me because the monument to Mrs. Robbie Key Garrett Carter, those words etched in ink on her obituary, say her fried fruit pies and chocolate pies were "delivered with a warm smile to her friends in the Carthage Community." Her *friends*. That she and Mr. Roy befriended me, encouraged my ministry, served me Sunday dinner and delectable pastries for months on end, and came to my ordination, is a grace to which I owe a fervent repentance, repentance like unto that of the woman to whom I proposed and joined my life behind the monument four decades ago.

Silver (Shoe) Anniversary

Jennie and I returned to Carthage a few times over the years to visit the church where I served as Pastor and where she played the piano for ten bucks, a free ride, and a wedding dress. Now our silver wedding anniversary is a distant memory. We spent it in grand fashion by flying to Anchorage, visiting church members who winter in Phoenix and summer in Alaska and taking a cruise down the Inner Passage.

Not all our anniversaries have been observed with such gusto. In fact, most of our anniversaries have been, well, underwhelming. We're able to laugh about them ... now.

Take our 10th anniversary, for instance. We lined up a babysitter, cleared our schedules in advance, and went out anticipating an evening commensurate with the occasion.

After a pleasant enough dinner, I turned to Jennie and asked, "Where now?"

She shrugged her shoulders. After an uncomfortable silence she deadpanned, "We really know how to do it up right, don't we?"

We ended up at Sam's Club shopping for luggage. We said

we'd tell everybody we went out to dinner and then to 'the Club' on our anniversary.

We laughed about that on our 24th anniversary gala that began with dinner and followed with our looking at each other and asking in unison, "Now what?" followed by "Sam's?" and then, "No, really. Where shall we go?"

We ended up walking across the street from the restaurant to a ritzy shopping plaza where our neighbors had opened up a fancy-schmancy shoe store. Over dinner at our house one night, they told us about their line of custom-made Italian shoes and accessories. Jennie and I being the Italian shoe connoisseurs we are told them we'd be sure and stop in the store when we were in the area. It would be the neighborly thing to do.

So, it being a beautiful night and us having time on our hands, we ambled over to Michelangelo's or DaVinci's or Botticelli's or whatever their shoe store is called. As soon as I crossed the threshold in my svelte Docksiders, I knew I was out of my league. I didn't even look to see what Jennie had on her feet, but the dapper salesman must have seen our pedestrian footwear and the out-of-our-league look in our eyes, recognized we weren't exactly prospective customers, and said, "It's all right to dream."

In no time we were back outside wondering where else we might go for our celebration. There was no Sam's Club nearby.

"There's a theater across the street," Jennie said. "Let's go see what's playing."

We did, but the next showings weren't scheduled to begin for an hour. By then, I would have begun my 9 p.m. turning-into-a-pumpkin routine that 24 years of marriage has not changed.

"How about gelato?" Jennie suggested.

Perfect! If we couldn't have Italian shoes, we could at least have Italian dessert. We cruised over to the gelato place with the moon roof of our aging Honda Accord open (romantic, huh?), ate our cups of gelato on the patio, joked about how "We really know how to do it up right, don't we?" and then headed home before the clock tolled Pumpkin Time. We were in bed by ten. I'm not sure what time it was in Rome.

The Resurrection Rant

I performed my first wedding at Carthage. It was for John and Lib's daughter Leanne. Lib made Jennie's wedding dress; I did her daughter's wedding.

I did my first funeral there, too. It was for Miz Ella Robinson, a long-time member of the church and mother of elder Kenneth Robinson. She died when I had been there all of four months. If I was unfit to lead *a cappella* singing, I was even less fit to preside at a funeral.

Having never been to a funeral, much less done one before, I turned to a friend. Ron was a Lutheran pastor who had returned to seminary to pursue a Ph.D. in Theology. Renown for launching into memorable, downright comical diatribes on everything from the woes of the Minnesota Viking football team to the idiosyncrasies of Scandinavian Lutherans, Ron had a salty style of communicating that never failed to enlighten as well as entertain.

With much hand-wringing, I shared with him my dilemma: someone in my congregation had died and I had been asked to do the funeral. What was I going to say?

Ron nearly came out of his chair. In fact, he did come out

of his chair. His body leaned toward me, his eyes widened, then he sprang to his feet and delivered a roundhouse rant the tone and content of which still rings in my ear.

"What are you going to say? What do you mean what are you going to say? You're gonna preach the resurrection! *What* do you think you're going to do? Talk about the friggin' weather?" With that, he plopped back down in his chair red-faced, spent.

Pastor Ron made his point. I needed no clarification. In the face of death, you talk about the resurrection. What a concept.

That's when I committed John 11:25 to memory: "Jesus said, 'I am the resurrection and the life. Those who believe in me, though they die, yet shall they live.'"

Since Miz Ella's funeral in October of 1982, I've now quoted John 11:25 at the beginning of 240 funerals.

I quoted Jesus' words at Miz Ella's funeral in 1982 when she died at the age of 82.

I quoted them at Mark Schmoll's funeral in 1986 when he died at the age of 26.

I quoted them to Mary and Mark whose first-born son Carl lived but two days and I quoted them to Hugh and Janet whose son Tim lived three decades longer before taking his own life.

I quoted Jesus' words to the friends and families of the half dozen AIDS patients to whom I ministered as a hospice volunteer for two and a half years in the early nineties who asked me to do their funerals.

I quoted Jesus' words at the gravesides of scores of people obviously beloved by their families and I quoted them at the graveside of a man whose son, when I asked him how he would remember his father, said disdainfully, "He was a son of a b-----!" Family members seated near him nodded their heads in agreement.

I quoted Jesus' words over the graves of people whose names I'll never forget and I quoted them at the grave of a man whose name nobody knew.

An undertaker in my Indiana congregation received custody of an unidentified homeless man's corpse. Wanting him to have a proper burial, the undertaker called and asked, "Would you come out to the cemetery and say a few words before we lower him into the ground?"

For a split second, I began to ponder what I was going to say, but the visage of an animated Lutheran pastor came to mind. He didn't have to say a word this time. I knew just what I'd say and I did. After John 11:25, I added a few words from the Psalmist: "Whither can I go from your spirit? Whither can I flee from your presence? If I take the wings of the morning and settle at the farthest limits of the sea, even there your hand shall lead me and your right hand shall hold me fast." (Psalm 139)

My funeral director parishioner said a few words of commendation. We stood together in silence for a few seconds, then turned and walked back to the hearse as the cemetery workers lowered the casket into the ground.

Bread, Cup, Pie, and Preserves

In the weeks before her death and Pastor Ron's resurrection rant, I took communion to Miz Ella's home. She attended worship for as long as she could. After the benediction, she could be counted on to extend the exact same invitation week in and week out: "Now Preacher, you just stop by this week and sit a spell with me. Got some homemade banana cream pie made fresh last night. A piece got your name on it. You be sure and stop by now, hear?"

Who could resist? Some Wednesdays I drove out to Carthage to make visits. When I stopped by Miz Ella's, she would be sitting on her sofa, pivoted to the left so that her good ear was aimed toward my armchair. In between bites of the homemade pie, we would "visit." In the weeks before she died when she could no longer serve me pie, I returned the favor by serving her a more traditional communion — bread and juice.

Miz Ella was a woman of faith. Eighty years of hymn singing, Bible reading, and weekly worship had framed her soul and she carried it well. Our visits ended the same way – "Now Preacher, you just read me Psalms 23 and 121, say a prayer, and I'll be much obliged." As I read the psalms her lips moved silently in unison with my every word. She knew them by heart. Upon the "Amen" at the end of my prayer, she would thank me and tell me she would look forward to communion next week when I was in town.

"Just knock and come right on in," she'd say, "You're family here."

During the week, I was serving as a student chaplain at a hospital in Nashville. At night I was on call and carried a beeper by which the hospital operator could reach me. One night the beeper went off at two in the morning. I jumped out of bed, stumbled across the darkened room to the telephone, and called in.

The hospital operator asked, "Would it be possible for you to bring a patient communion?"

"At two o'clock in the morning?"

"Yes," she said, "She's scheduled for surgery in a couple of days, can't sleep, and asked the nurse if the Chaplain could come in for prayer and communion."

"O.K.," I said, "I'm on my way." I threw on a pair of pants and a shirt, tied my tie, and made my way to the car. I stopped at a 24-hour convenience store for grape juice and bread (other customers were buying beer or cigarettes) and made my way to the hospital.

After finding the room, I walked in and introduced myself. She told me she was "worried about being cut on." We talked. I read Scripture. We prayed. I served her communion.

As she handed me the empty cup she asked, "Where are you from?"

"I'm originally from Ohio," I said.

To which she responded flatly, "I knew you weren't one of us."

Ouch.

I thought we had had communion. Evidently not. On my way to the elevators, I was aware that the grape juice had left a bad taste in my mouth.

Not one of us?

Miz Ella died not long after that. The day before she died as we gathered around her hospital bed she rallied long enough to speak to her son and daughter. She saw me and whispered, "You stop by tomorrow morning and I'll make us some fresh biscuits and homemade strawberry preserves and we'll visit for a spell."

What I heard her say was "You're one of us."

To this day, I speak loud enough to be heard clearly by her good ear at ten paces. I will take communion to anybody anywhere at the drop of a hat. And I've got this gut-level hunch that in Psalm 23 where it says "Thou preparest a table before me" that table has on it homemade banana cream pie, fresh biscuits, strawberry preserves, bread, and juice.

Saddam and Samal

Samal was also told he was not one of us, much to the displeasure of his fiancée's grandmother, Margaret Westmoreland.

Back in August of 1990, not long after Iraq's invasion of neighboring Kuwait, I was stopped at an intersection behind a car sporting a bumper sticker that read KICK SADDAM'S ASS. That the driver thought nothing of pasting profanity on the back of his Cadillac was one thing, but that he was articulating a sentiment shared by legions of others was another.

I was first acquainted with Saddam Hussein in 1985 while at Carthage. Iraq was in the midst of a long and bloody war with Iran back then and as far as U.S. foreign policy was concerned, "Any enemy of my enemy the Ayatollah is a friend of mine." Hence, our "friendship" with Iraq and Saddam.

Samal knew another side of Saddam. He had fled Iraq during one of the waves of persecution Saddam had visited upon his native Kurdish people, persecution that included the unleashing of chemical weapons upon Kurdish men, women, and children. Though it meant putting his life at risk, Samal decided to flee, eventually arriving in Nashville.

In Nashville, Samal worked at menial jobs during the day while taking English classes at night from Margaret Westmoreland's granddaughter. In time, Laura and Samal began dating. They had dinner with Jennie and me. When they visited Laura's grandmother, Margaret, in Carthage, they attended worship.

During their courtship, some townsfolk approached Margaret with raised eyebrows, saying they had seen her granddaughter with an Arab (pronounced with a long A followed by *rab* as in rabbit, with the accent on the first syllable). To which feisty Margaret, then in her mid-eighties, barked, "I'll have you know Samal is a prince of a young man!" and "That's my granddaughter you're talking about!" followed by "Those two love one another and if that's the case then it's fine with me and God bless 'em both!" and ending with, "Now have you got a problem with that?"

At which point her interlocutors decided they didn't have a problem after all, whereupon they bid Miss Margaret a good day and walked backward off her front porch with their tails between their legs until they backed all the way to their cars.

Samal and Laura married and gave birth to a lovely daughter, the most beautiful great-granddaughter in the whole world in Margaret's eyes. A few years later, Samal became a U.S. citizen.

All of which brings me back to the fella driving the Cadillac with the bumper sticker advocating the annihilation of Saddam. To accomplish his goal, would he have countenanced the death of thousands of Iraqi troops? Judging by the language of his bumper sticker, undoubtedly so. Would the death of Iraqi civilians have been acceptable? I suspect so. Would he have approved of such carnage even if it included a

Kurdish couple in Iraq treasuring a photo of their son standing next to his wife holding in his arms a granddaughter they longed to see?

In the face of zealots who would have loved nothing better than to do to Romans what the man in the Cadillac wanted to do to Saddam, Jesus stood on a Mount and said, "Love your enemies and pray for those who persecute you." I can't help but wonder how those words translate into foreign policy or what they'd look like in boldface on a bumper sticker and what it means that such a sticker wouldn't sell near as well as the one I saw on the Cadillac.

Cana in Reverse

I do know this: Samal was welcome at Carthage Christian Church. Our front door, arms, and communion table were open to all.

In addition to preaching, my other primary responsibility at the church was to prepare communion. Communion preparation was rather routine: open the refrigerator, take out a bottle of chilled Welch's grape juice, plop twenty communion cups into the tray, and fill each one three-quarters full.

No problem, except for one Sunday. Jennie and I got to the church and turned on the lights. I proceeded to the refrigerator and found we had at most an ounce of grape juice left in the bottom of the Welch's bottle. I gave Jennie the keys to the car and sent her off to the grocery store on a Welch's grape juice run. She came back empty-handed. The grocery store was closed on Sundays until Noon.

I thought to myself, "Where is a broken blue law when you need one?"

I remembered there was a 24-hour convenience store on the other side of the bridge on the way into town. Jennie drove over. They were open (Thank goodness they didn't honor the Sabbath!). They sold everything from Swiss army knives and Hank Williams, Jr. eight-track tapes to sausage biscuits and moon pies, but no grape juice. Jennie said she spotted Grape Nehi in the cooler, but she didn't figure the folks would want any carbonation in their cups so she passed and came on back to the church.

By now folks were arriving for Sunday School hour. I asked them as they came in if they happened to have any grape juice at home. None did. I concluded that most people do not drink grape juice at any time other than Sunday mornings at church. I had offers of apple, tomato, orange, cranberry, and prune juice (multiple offers), but no grape juice.

I scurried over to Mr. Bill's house, our head elder who lived two doors north of the church and told him of our predicament. Billie Ruth stood in the background listening in. I explained how I had done everything possible to secure some grape juice but had run out of options as far as I could see. He said that as far as he could see we were sure in for a sorry worship service without communion. I returned to the church dejected.

Billie Ruth appeared several minutes later with a brown bag. She opened it and handed its contents to me. Someone had given Mr. Bill a bottle of wine as a Christmas present years ago. She told me that though she and Mr. Bill never drank, Mr. Bill had opened the gift back then "as a courtesy" and took a sip. "It didn't agree with him," she said, so he put the cap back on (Yes, cap and not cork) and put it on the top shelf of the pantry where it had sat all these years until she remembered it was there, got it down, and was now offering it for communion. The bottle delivered into my hands, she turned and walked out to the sanctuary.

Have you ever seen a bottle of wine that has been sitting open in a dark pantry for years? It is not dressed appropriately for church. Neither does its contents offer a pleasing fragrance unto the Lord. I screwed the lid back on the offending offering, put it back in its bag, and set it in a distant corner.

With worship about to begin, I took the ounce or so of grape juice we had left and added enough water to fill seventeen communion cups. You've heard of water into wine? This was Cana in reverse. We communed that morning with rose-colored water that had just the slightest aroma of grapes. No one said a word.

I gave Billie Ruth's brown bag back to her after the service. I thanked her for her thoughtfulness, told her we didn't need it after all and suggested she and Mr. Bill didn't need it, either.

Here's to You, Mr. Robertson

I guess we could have used 7-Up that morning in Carthage. That was the sacrament of choice every Saturday evening when I communed with Joe Robinson.

Mr. Robertson lived alone and was dying of lung cancer. I visited him as a volunteer for Hospice. Those were in my pre-Carthage days when I thought I wanted to be a hospital chaplain rather than a parish minister. I couldn't imagine having to prepare a sermon every week for the rest of my life.

We were a study in contrasts, Mr. Robertson and I. At 22, my whole life was ahead of me. At 75, his life was drawing to a close. I called him Mr. Robertson out of respect. He called me Mr. David out of the prescribed deferential politeness expected of an African-American man toward a white man fifty years his junior.

I told him numerous times, "Just call me David, Mr. Robertson" to which he'd reply, "Yes, Mr. David."

Over three months, Mr. Robertson and I became friends. His one delight was 7-Up. He said it soothed his parched throat. So, I'd show up on his doorstep every Saturday evening with a six-pack. We'd sip 7-Up and talk. We'd talk about fishing, his work on the railroad, and his late wife. When he learned I was studying to be a preacher, a sparkle came to eyes that were sunken and yellowed. Between coughs and wheezes, he exclaimed, "The gospel of the Lord! Yes, sir, Mr. David, you just preach the gospel of the Lord. Yes, indeed!"

One Saturday evening I told him a little church in Carthage had asked me to be their minister. Well, they didn't exactly ask me, they *told* me. I had substituted one Sunday for a graduating senior at Carthage and preached my one sermon. The following Wednesday someone knocked on my door and told me I had a call on the house phone downstairs. It was Mr. Bill.

"David Shirey," he said, "we had a congregational meeting after you left last Sunday and we have called you to be the next pastor of Carthage Christian Church."

"But Mr. Read," I said, "I wasn't looking to become your next pastor. I was just filling in."

To which he responded, "David Shirey, that wasn't a question, that was a statement, son."

Hence my call to Carthage.

I told Mr. Robertson that I didn't know if I could do it, how standing behind that pulpit with seventeen people looking at me made my knees knock and my stomach churn and besides, how would I come up with something to say every week?

As I lamented my call, he smiled a toothy grin and said aloud, "Oh, the gospel of the Lord! Mr. David, just you preach the gospel of the Lord."

So I did. Or, I should say with Mr. Robertson's help I did. For each week leading up to the Sunday I was to preach, I agonized over what to say. On Saturday night before each sermon was to be delivered, I showed up on Mr. Robertson's doorstep with a six-pack of 7-Up in one hand and the sermon in the other.

"Do you mind if I run this sermon by you?" I asked.

He would smile broadly, shake his head from side to side, and break out into a laugh that in turn produced a coughing spell. I would pour him a 7-Up on the rocks and hand it to him. The cough would abate and I'd launch into my sermon.

He sipped his soothing tonic and listened as I stammered along, encouraging me with audible Amens along the way.

When I finished, I looked up and asked, "What do you think?"

All I remember are the jaundiced yellow eyes, the toothy grin, and the raspy refrain, "Yes, sir, you just preach the gospel of the Lord, Mr. David. Yes sir."

Every Saturday evening until the day he died, I'd show up on Mr. Joe Robertson's doorstep with Sunday's sermon and a six-pack of 7–Up.

I see the sparkle in the eye. I see the broad smile. And from time to time as I go through Sunday's sermon on a Saturday night, I hear the whispered reassurance, "The gospel of the Lord! Yes, sir, Mr. David, you just preach the gospel of the Lord. Yes, indeed!"

Here's to you, Mr. Robertson.

Communion Confusion

I got my first taste of taking communion to the infirm from another Mr. Joe — an elder in my home church named Joe Ross. He doted on my dad when my dad was just a kid and took me under his wing as well.

Once a month, members of our high school youth group would accompany the elders on home communion. We'd go out two-by-two to our congregation's shut-ins and hospitalized. My partner would always be Joe Ross. As we walked to his car he never failed to remind me how he knew my father when "he was just a little whippersnapper" and how I was surely growing up fast.

"What are they feeding you, Shirey?" he'd ask. "You're gonna be a big 'un!" Off we'd go on our rounds. One Sunday we went to a nursing home, a sprawling complex at which we had several members. When we arrived at the central lounge a half dozen folks were waiting for us. Several others arrived shortly thereafter. Mr. Ross took a quick headcount, saw we were missing one, and sent me off in search of her.

Not knowing my way around, I stopped at a nurses' station and asked for directions.

"Down C Wing to the blue carpet, then right until you pass the nurses' station. Turn left down D Wing. It'll be the fourth door on your left, bed two."

Or something like that. I followed directions as best I could and entered a room where I found a woman in a wheelchair, head in hands. The curtains were drawn.

"Good morning," I said, "I've come to take you to communion. Ready to go?"

No response. I remember the woman's head slowly rising from her hands and her looking up at me with a quizzical expression. I couldn't tell whether she was surprised, confused, or had just awoken from a nap. Not knowing what else to do, I walked behind her wheelchair and proceeded to push her down the winding corridors until we reached the spot where the other dozen or so were waiting for us.

I pushed her into place, walked over to Mr. Ross, and whispered, "I got lost."

"That's all right," he whispered back, "but who's that you brought back with you?"

"What do you mean?"

"That's not Mrs. Whitfield. But we'll get her later. We need to start."

"Sorry."

"No need to apologize. This is the Lord's Table. All are welcome."

Had I had the late-night communion experience I was to have in the Nashville hospital years later, I might have whispered sarcastically, "But she's not one of us!"

Mr. Joe handled the service from there. He filled the folks in on what was happening at the church. He introduced his sixteen-year-old associate ("Now young Shirey here is a fine young man. I knew his daddy when he was just a boy ... "). He then said a prayer and the Words of Institution. I helped him pass out the bread and cup.

After the service, I rolled our guest in the wheelchair back to her room. Embarrassed at my gaffe, I fumbled for what to say. The poor lady was sitting in her room minding her own business when some teenager bolted in and hijacked her wheelchair to a communion service! I began to apologize but had no sooner begun to talk than I noticed she was crying.

"Young man," she said, "Before you came in I was praying that I could have communion today. I haven't seen anyone from my church for such a long time that I had given up hope. So I prayed that I could have communion. I was praying when you came into the room. I couldn't believe my ears when you came in and said you'd come to take me to communion. Thank you, young man. Thank you."

She extended her hand, gave mine a squeeze, and smiled.

Me? I was spooked. I went back to Mr. Ross and told him the whole story, how I had not followed the nurse's directions properly, how I'd commandeered that poor lady's wheelchair and brought her to our gathering, how she'd cried, and how she told me she had been praying for communion when I came in.

"I can't believe I went to the wrong room and brought the wrong lady back for communion," I said

"Shirey," Mr. Joe said, "did you say *wrong* room? Did you say *wrong* lady?"

I nodded my head.

"Think about it," he said, "Think about it."

Older and somewhat wiser now, I still think about it. "God can draw straight lines with crooked sticks," is how I've heard it, even guiding gangly teenagers down crooked corridors to contribute to holy ends.

Mr. Joe's Benediction

Joe Ross changed my life. As a teenager, I was gangly, indeed — a 6'4" fence post with acne. My height did me no good. I got cut from the basketball team and was too skinny for the football team, so I went out for the track team (nobody ever got cut from the track team) and ended up running the distance races — the mile and two-mile — without success. I didn't think very highly of myself because I knew no one else did. So I slunk around stoop-shouldered, head at half-mast.

During those years, I was a reluctant attendee at Central Christian Church in Warren, Ohio. I had a choice every Sunday morning. I could stay at home with Dad and sweep the basement, wash and wax the car, and do yard work or I could go to church with Mom. In my mind, going to church was the lesser of two evils.

During my freshman year, an older man in the congregation began what became a weekly ritual. He would seek me out after worship where I'd usually be found in wallflower fashion leaning against the back wall waiting for my mother. He'd come up beside me, put his arm around my shoulder, and say, "David Shirey, you're something special and don't let anybody tell you any different." It was Mr. Joe.

I brushed it off at first as old man stuff — Yeah, Pops, right. But as the weekly ritual continued something began to happen. I started to stand up a little straighter and put my shoulders back a little more. He sought me out throughout my high school years, rested his yarmulke of a hand on my shoulder each and every Sunday, and pronounced his benediction into my ear: "David Shirey, you're something special and don't let anybody tell you any different."

Low self-image meets Made-in-the-image-of-God. I began to hear through Mr. Joe's voice the voice of the One who looked down from heaven upon Jesus the day of his baptism and said, "You are my beloved son; with you I am well pleased" (Mark 1:11). I heard through that elder's voice the voice of the Ancient of Days who had said through Jeremiah, "I have loved you with an everlasting love" (Jeremiah 31:3).

I graduated high school in late May. The Sunday before I was to head out-of-state to college, I stood in the back of the sanctuary with a demonstrably more upright posture. I was waiting for Mr. Joe's benediction.

I looked around the emptying sanctuary. Where was he? Then I spotted him. I looked across the sanctuary and saw with my own eyes Mr. Joe standing next to some freshman kid. Short. Squat. Geeky-looking. Jeff somebody or other. Then I saw Mr. Ross put his arm around that kid, squeeze his shoulder — and I could read his lips as clear as day — he said, "Jeff, you're somebody special and don't you let anybody tell you any different."

I thought to myself, "You two-timer! What's up with that?

Do you do that to every kid?"

Which is when Mr. Joe met my eyes from the other side of the room, smiled broadly, and winked.

Late that fall at college, I received a letter from home. I took it up to my dorm room, sat on the bed, and opened it. Inside there was a newspaper clipping. I unfolded it and read it. At the top, there was a photograph of a kindly visage I recognized. Beneath it, the text read something like, "Joseph Ross, 83, of Warren, Ohio, died Wednesday at Trumbull Memorial Hospital after a brief illness. Mr. Ross was an Elder at Central Christian Church and a friend and advocate of this community's youth. He is survived by ...."

I sat on my bed in my dorm room and cried.

We have a kid named Sam that has been coming to our church recently. One of our elders has sort of adopted him and brings him along. Sam comes from a rough background, I understand. There are all sorts of family issues, I'm told.

I make it a point to find him on Sunday mornings. I sidle up next to him, cuff him on the shoulder, and tell him "You're something special, Sam, and don't you let anybody tell you any different."

The Turkey Trot

Kenneth Robinson was an elder like Mr. Joe Ross. Carthage Christian Church had three elders– Mr. Bill, eighteen-wheeler John Collette, and Kenneth. With John on the road a lot, I had the privilege of standing alongside Kenneth every other Sunday at the Lord's Table.

I had the privilege of running alongside him, too. At age 50, Kenneth suffered a heart attack. The doctor gave him the "Change your diet and lifestyle or else" lecture and Kenneth took his words to heart … and legs. He took up running.

What began as a few hundred yards of huffing and puffing turned into double-digit miles through Smith County's rolling county roads. Forrest Gump had nothing on Elder Robinson. Ten-mile jaunts became a gleefully-anticipated part of Kenneth's rule of life to the point that by the time I met him, then in his mid-sixties, he was running marathons (26.2 miles) and winning medals for his age group.

I was a runner in my day. In fact, I may hold the school record at Howland High for third-place finishes in a career. Every race someone from our team and someone from the other team would cross the finish line well before me. The runner-up to the runner-up, that's me.

I've kept running all these years, though not competitively (there's no room in my trophy case for more bronze medals). I run for the calm and quiet. It's a spiritual discipline. The author of the 23rd Psalm was a distance runner. "He leadeth me beside still waters, he restoreth my soul" is the giveaway. Nothing is more restorative of body, mind, and spirit than a long run.

For the two and a half years I was at Carthage, Kenneth said we needed to run together. Finally, we did. We registered for a 10k (6.2 mile) race in Nashville. It was near Thanksgiving and was called "The Turkey Trot." Kenneth and I lined up together, but that was the closest I would be to the man forty years my senior the entire race. Kenneth raced, but this turkey trotted — if trotting is even the word. I was out of shape on a hilly course on an unseasonably warm day which brought another verse from Psalm 23 to mind: "Even though I [trot] through the valley of the shadow of death ...."

I wanted to stop and walk, but since my goal was to finish the race without stopping that would have been tantamount to quitting, so I pressed on. I played mind games: just get to the top of this hill and it's all downhill from there. I did ... but it wasn't. I'd crest the hill, thighs burning, lungs heaving, only to see another monster of asphalt rising before me.

More mind games: When the thought of quitting returned, I'd huff, "Get thee behind me, Satan!" That'd be good for another hill or two.

I'd say to myself, "Since we are surrounded by so great a cloud of witnesses, let us run with perseverance the race that is set before us." But there were no witnesses along the route — I could stop and walk and no one would see me ... *Wait a minute!* "Get thee behind me, Satan!" On I trotted.

Then this. When I was still a mile or so from the finish line, Kenneth appeared. He had crested a hill a hundred yards ahead of me and was coming my way. He had finished the race, turned around, and come all the way back to spur me along. With him at my side offering words of encouragement, "You can do it, David. Keep it up. You're gonna do it!" I finished. Without him, I couldn't have.

Fast-forward now twenty-five years to church-planting days. For four long years, our building plans were quashed by the City of Scottsdale over floodplain issues. That's a laugh line, by the way. Smack dab in the middle of the Sonoran Desert and our plans are relegated to City Hall's design deep freeze because we're supposedly in a future Sonoran Swamp.

That was just one of our setbacks. Many times I pondered stopping and walking away. But every time I reached that point I glimpsed Kenneth on the horizon, coming my way out of my past and out of my future, coming alongside me with an encouraging word to keep me keepin' on.

In the Bible, the Greek word for God's Holy Spirit is *Paraclete*. It means literally, "to come alongside."

The city finally approved our drainage plans for when the one-hundred-year flood comes. We're required to post signs in the parking lot amidst the rattlesnake holes and cactus warning motorists that in the event of a flood, the Coolwater Christian Church parking lot will be waist-deep in the Coolwater River. I can live with that.

What I can't live with is the prospect of having to persevere through adversity without the encouragement of certain others like Kenneth who have come alongside us. Surrounded by so great a cloud of witnesses, we persevere, cross the finish line, and receive the victor's crown: a building permit to construct an ark in a flood plain.

Harry's Altar Call

The late North Carolina Baptist preacher Carlyle Marney ("A voice like God's, only deeper") called them "our balcony people." He was referring to the folks in our lives who have been our encouragers, the mere memory of whom is all we need to renew our strength. Kenneth was one. So was his wife Frances Sue. So were Mr. Bill and Billie Ruth, Margaret Westmoreland, Pastor Ron, Miz Ella, and my Mr. Joes — Robertson and Ross. I count all of them among my balcony people.

I number Harry and Ova, Aunt Hazel, Chet and Edna, and Marjorie on that list as well. Their stories, too, have risen from the ashes.

We have a dozen or so snowbirds in our Arizona new church start. The desert is rife with them—- folks who winter in Phoenix but have the good sense to migrate to cooler climes when summer temperatures get stuck in triple digits. Harry and Ova were our Carthage Christian snowbirds, wintering in east central Tennessee before heading back to east central Illinois for the summer.

Harry had a wonderful sense of humor. With his elfin

appearance and infectious laugh, he was good company at the pre-worship coffee/Bible study hour. But since "What goes in must come out" is a biological truth, Harry's intake of pre-worship coffee led to his excusing himself during worship for relief, including the Sunday of John and Lib's supposed anniversary.

Robert Burns opined "the best laid schemes o' mice an' men," things don't always turn out the way we hoped they might. When we were at our North Carolina church in the 1990s, one Sunday we made big plans for (drum roll, please): *Church School Celebration Sunday.* Jennie and I rented a helium tank, inflated fifty balloons, designed a couple dozen official-looking Certificates of Appreciation, and inscribed them with our best amateur calligraphy skills.

No children showed up. None. Zero. Will Rogers once joked about what would happen if they called a war and nobody came. Well, what about calling a *Church School Celebration Sunday* and having no Church School celebrants? I couldn't help but notice that toward the end of the service, a pair of our previously high-flying balloons were floating half-mast as if in mourning. They, too, were deflated.

It reminded me of my very first no-show Sunday. It was the spring of '83. I had been pastor at Carthage for nine months or so. John and Lib Collette asked me if I would consider preaching a special sermon commemorating their upcoming 35th wedding anniversary.

"Something on love would be mighty nice," John said.

I agreed and prepared a sermon on three and a half decades of marital bliss. I made the sixty-mile trek to Carthage on John and Lib's anniversary Sunday, love sermon in hand, but John and Lib didn't show up. No word as to why. I should have realized right then the day was ill-fated, but the best was yet to come.

I launched into my sermon, a syrupy, sentimental soliloquy on love, and was preaching my way through it when Harry made his weekly move. He rose from his pew, made his way to the center aisle, then walked to the front in altar-call fashion, up the steps of the chancel, and past the pulpit within an arm's length of me. He then opened the door behind the pulpit that led from the sanctuary into the small classroom with an adjoining restroom and closed the door behind him, disappearing from view. He explained to me once in great detail the medical reasons for his intermittent departures from the sanctuary, so I had come to expect his jaunts that beat a path past the pulpit and back again once nature's 'altar call' had been alleviated.

I did not, however, expect one of Harry's altar calls to punctuate my love sermon quite the way it did. After he passed by the pulpit that Sunday en route to his desired destination, I pressed on toward the cloying climax of my marital bliss sermon in honor of the absentee honorees. Then it happened. Just as I reached my final crescendo, Harry flushed the toilet.

Are you old enough to remember episodes of *All In The Family* when Archie Bunker flushed the upstairs commode? Do you remember the ruckus it raised in the living room downstairs? That's the closest analogy I can think of to the commotion raised in the Carthage sanctuary. So it was that just as I was pressing toward my sermonic Amen, Harry hit the magical lever, simultaneously drowning out my voice, flushing my sentimental thoughts down the drain, and sending 77-year-old Billie Ruth Read into fits of muffled laughter in the front pew.

I stopped, smirked, guffawed, and then chuckled out loud while drawing my sermon to a merciful close. Harry then opened the door, shuffled past the pulpit, down the center aisle, and took his seat in the third pew oblivious to what had happened.

I never asked John and Lib why they didn't make it to church that Sunday. Nor did any of us ever say a word to Harry. Nor did I ask the kids why they didn't show up for Church School Celebration Sunday years later.

The way I look at it now, that sappy sermon needed to be curbed sooner rather than later. Thank goodness for Harry who, though he has long since gone on to his eternal reward, stands now among my balcony people, his leprechaun laughter poking a much-needed hole in my self-importance, his flesh and blood realities bringing a much-needed counterbalance to my over-inflated rhetoric.

Truth be told, though, I'm glad the restrooms in our present congregation's first-phase multipurpose building will be to the rear of the worship space.

Aunt Hazel

Whereas Harry missed the end of my love sermon, Aunt Hazel missed the entire worship service. It was the Spring weekend when Daylight Savings Time ended. Though there were all the normal reminders to "Move your clocks ahead one hour before going to bed Saturday night," Aunt Hazel missed the memo.

I was standing at the chancel steps at the end of the service when the doors to the sanctuary opened and Aunt Hazel shuffled in. I had just extended the Invitation and was announcing the Closing Hymn when her eyes met mine. She later explained that she thought she was just a few minutes late, that the Invitation was the Call to Worship and the Closing Hymn was the Opening Hymn, so she gave me a rather sheepish "Oops! Sorry-for-being-late" look and proceeded toward her seat.

As we sang the Closing Hymn that Aunt Hazel thought was the Opening Hymn she tip-toed down the side aisle and stepped into her pew, eight back from the front on the right-hand side, nodded to those standing around her, and got herself situated just in time to join in singing the "Amen" after the hymn.

With that, Aunt Hazel reverently closed her eyes and bowed her head with the rest of the congregation for a prayer she figured was the Invocation but was in fact the Benediction. As the "Amen" to the Benediction was spoken, she plopped herself down in her pew and settled in for what she figured was going to be the Welcome and Announcements but much to her bewilderment turned out to be the mass exodus of everyone seated around her (as much as the departure of fifteen people can be said to be a mass exodus).

As the congregation filed out of their pews and mingled in the center aisle, Aunt Hazel sat in her pew with a befuddled look on her face. At that point, someone walked over to her pew, leaned down, whispered something, and then pointed to their watch at which point Aunt Hazel raised her hands, covered her face, and broke out in a rippling of giggles that caused her whole body to jiggle.

I walked over to where she was sitting and before I could say a word, she said, "David, I jes' plumb fergot. Oh my, my, my. I jes' plumb fergot!"

It was just about then that Kenneth Robinson, Aunt Hazel's nephew and chauffeur, finally made his way through the front door after having parked the car.

"Oh, Kenneth," Aunt Hazel said, chuckling, "You'll never guess in a million years what we done …."

Kenneth was a good sport with his aging aunt and her forgetfulness. He and I were invited to Aunt Hazel's one Sunday after worship for Sunday dinner. For weeks leading up to our dinner date, Aunt Hazel told Kenneth and me to "save our appetites" for a home-cooked meal.

Did we like chicken?

Yes, Ma'am, we did.

Well, she was going to bake the preacher and her nephew a chicken.

Did we like mashed potatoes?

Yes, Ma'am, we did.

Well, she whipped her potatoes just so and made a tasty gravy on top of 'em.

Did we like homemade biscuits served hot and fresh with melted butter running down the sides?

"Stop it, Aunt Hazel," Kenneth pleaded, "You're making me hungry and dinner's still two weeks off."

She then pointed a playful finger at us, giggled the way she did, and proceeded to name yet more menu items.

Kenneth confided in me the Sunday morning of the long-anticipated feast that he couldn't recall the last time Aunt Hazel had done much cooking but he was glad to see the interest she was taking in preparing Sunday dinner for us. He added, "No telling how it'll turn out."

He was right. When we got to her house after closing up the church, Aunt Hazel showed us to the dining room table and invited us to have a seat. A dish of mashed potatoes and a side dish of gravy were on the table along with a plate of sliced white bread and a stick of butter.

"I'll be right back with your coffee — just perked it fresh!" Aunt Hazel said as she headed back to the kitchen.

Pointing to the sliced bread, Kenneth smiled and whispered, "She must have forgotten the homemade biscuits."

That wasn't all she forgot. She forgot to cook the chicken. Kenneth was the first to make the discovery. When told by her nephew of the still-thawing main course, Aunt Hazel put her hand over her mouth, raised both eyebrows, disappeared into the kitchen without saying a word, and then reappeared in the doorway.

"David and Kenneth," she said, "You'll never guess in a million years what I done. I put the chicken in the oven a while ago and I forgot to turn it on. Oh my, my, my. I jes' plumb fergot!"

For the next hour, the three of us sipped hot coffee in Aunt Hazel's front room as we waited for the chicken to cook. During the hour we waited, Aunt Hazel regaled us with stories of her childhood, courtship, and fifty-year marriage. Her memory of those distant years undimmed, she recounted details that caused her nephew Kenneth to shake his head in wonder.

In time, the mashed potatoes and gravy were reheated and served piping hot along with a rather tasty roasted chicken. As we ate, Kenneth said, "Aunt Hazel, you sure can put out a spread. This sure is some fine chicken!"

"You outdid yourself, Aunt Hazel!" I added. "You make a fine boat of gravy, if I may say so myself."

She smiled and chuckled, "You boys!"

It was an afternoon of bountiful food and memories at Aunt Hazel's.

I haven't forgotten.

Chet's Mandolin

Going from Aunt Hazel's cold chicken to Edna Paris's biscuits and gravy was going from one extreme to the other.

Chet and Edna Paris lived on a winding Smith County road in a cozy home they had designed and built by themselves in the years following Chet's retirement. Edna could cook up the best plate of homemade biscuits with sausage gravy you ever put in your mouth and Chet never tired of bragging about them. Chet claimed that when he first set eyes on Edna he took a liking to her but when he tasted her sausage gravy and homemade biscuits he fell in love.

I fell in love with those biscuits and gravy myself, not to mention the liking I took to Chet and Edna. On any number of Wednesdays, I'd get an early start from Nashville, head to Carthage, and stop at the Paris's for breakfast. We three would eat together and while we ate we'd talk about whatever came up.

Chet's boyhood came up once.

"Now lemme tell ya," he said, "I was borned in a holler over yonder. Weren't no 'lectric or running water back in those days …."

Another time the subject of music came up. Chet said, "Holt on a minute while I go git somethin'." He came back with a pear-shaped stringed instrument and asked me if I knew what it was.

"A mandolin," I said, placing the emphasis on the last syllable.

"Yep," he said, "it's a mandolin all right," with emphasis on the first syllable.

Then he shook it. It made a rattling sound. He asked me if I knew what it was. I did not.

"It's got rattlesnake rattles in it," he said. He then extracted one of the little buggers and showed me. According to Chet, the rattles gave a more resonant tone to the mandolin. Whether it was true or not, I don't know, but I do know that Chet Paris could play that mandolin like nobody's business. Right there in the kitchen that day he played a couple of tunes.

He asked me if I liked Merle Haggard. He said he was "particular to 'ol Merle," whereupon he launched into "I'm Just an Okie from Muskogee." When he was done, he told me how he used to play in a four-piece bluegrass band years back and how he loved gospel music. Then, without even asking if I'd like to hear some, he leaned back in his chair, closed his eyes, and sang a gospel song.

As he did, I noticed Edna looking at Chet with the same admiring gaze he used on her when she served up the sausage gravy. There I sat at a kitchen table inside of a house made by a couple who were still very much in love, eating biscuits and gravy, drinking fresh coffee, listening to a man "from a yonder holler" sing gospel tunes with his rattlesnake-seasoned mandolin. Call it a pastoral privilege.

A few years later, Jennie and I received a Christmas card that said Chet had died. The card featured the angels serenading the shepherds. The shepherds stand there, awe written across their faces, listening to the anthem being played for them by the heavenly host. The angels are playing a bluegrass piece, I'm sure, and one of them is grinning broadly, strumming his mandolin.

Marjorie's Christmas Party

Marjorie lived alone with two big, smelly dogs in an A-frame overlooking the reservoir. After her husband died and was laid to rest in Arlington National Cemetery, Marjorie decided it was time for a change, so she sold her house, bought a trailer, hitched it up to the rear end of her Riviera, and headed south. She eventually pulled off I-40 in Tennessee east of Nashville because she liked the way it looked there. The exit sign on the interstate said CARTHAGE and that was where Marjorie and her dogs settled down in the A-frame overlooking the reservoir.

Marjorie stuck out like a sore thumb in Carthage. She spoke a mile a minute in a heavy Brooklyn accent and smoked long brown cigarettes. With her blazing red hair, bright red lipstick, and fashionable clothes, she just didn't fit in with the locals who spoke a mile an hour and favored clothing from the J.C. Penney catalog. So, even though she joined the Christian Church and the Senior Citizens Club of Smith County and a batch of other do-good organizations, Marjorie was on the outside looking in.

We had a potluck supper not long after Marjorie joined

the church. The locals brought the standard fare of fried chicken, green beans, mashed potatoes, and biscuits. Marjorie hauled in an industrial-sized baking pan filled with chicken cacciatore and a gallon jug of burgundy. By the looks people gave Marjorie when she pronounced the name of the dish she was carrying and hoisted the jug of wine, you would have thought she'd come to church buck-naked. No one knew what was in the pan ("Some kind of Eye-talian chicken," someone sniffed) so they didn't touch it. Everyone knew what was in the jug – so they didn't touch that, either. So Marjorie ended up taking her chicken cacciatore and burgundy back home with her. Both were untouched and she felt unwanted.

She gave the Seniors Club a try. They met in the basement of the Smith County Courthouse on Thursdays and played gin rummy and bingo and quilted and then had a lunch of fried chicken, green beans, mashed potatoes, and biscuits. One day Marjorie suggested that instead of cards and crafts, they have poetry readings and perhaps a slide show on Shakespeare's England. The Senior Club looked at Marjorie like she had come to play cards buck-naked. Again she felt unwanted. No one came out and said, "You're not one of us," but they could have. She didn't belong.

One Advent Marjorie gave me a call. She had an idea. I confess that without even hearing what it was I cringed. She wanted to throw a Christmas party for "the boys" at the Veterans Hospital in Murfreesboro. Marjorie's husband was in the service. He'd been hospitalized in the VA up in Baltimore before he died and she wanted to do something for "the boys" who were in the hospital.

It was a cold and wet night when I made the drive from

Nashville to Murfreesboro. Marjorie was waiting for me. The trunk of the Riviera was crammed with food and festive decorations. I was amazed at the spread she had prepared including plates of delicate hors d'oeuvres, a tasty punch with a Santa Claus ice mold afloat in it, and about twelve dozen cookies. All of it was homemade. It was from Marjorie to "the boys."

There was one problem. The nursing staff wasn't expecting us. Marjorie hadn't called or anything. She just figured she'd show up and surprise everyone. Which she did. The nurses didn't know what to make of the redhead with the long brown cigarettes who commenced putting up streamers in the lounge while singing "We Wish You a Merry Christmas" to guys in green bathrobes who were watching *Family Feud*. I started to explain what was going on and just when I thought I was making some headway, Marjorie plugged in the record player she had brought, threw a Glenn Miller Band album on the turntable, and proceeded to ask one of the guys in the green bathrobes if he wanted to dance. He did. Thus began what turned out to be quite a Christmas party in the Mental Health Ward of the Veterans Hospital in Murfreesboro, Tennessee.

As the evening wore on, Marjorie handed me a garbage bag and told me, "Go put it on!" Being in a military institution, I followed orders. Slipping into the Men's Room nearby, I opened the bag and spilled the contents out on the floor: a Santa Claus costume Marjorie had rented for the night.

Everybody laughed at the long, lanky Santa that emerged from the restroom and when Marjorie told everyone present I was her preacher, they all laughed some more. We partied for a couple of hours that night, Marjorie, the nurses, a few orderlies, the green bathrobed residents of Building C-3, and me in Santa Claus gear.

When we left, Marjorie was thanked profusely. Everyone begged her to return for New Year's Eve. She was wanted there.

That's about the last time I saw Marjorie. For all I know, she may still be living in her A-frame on the reservoir with her two big, smelly dogs, driving her Riviera, smoking long brown cigarettes, and throwing parties for outcasts.

For as long as I live I may never run into anyone quite as odd as Marjorie, nor anyone whose love for God and neighbor is greater. The true saints of God always stick out like sore thumbs. They never fit in here. But when God's Kingdom comes, they'll fit in.

Guess who'll feel out of place?

The Murphys are Coming

The year of Marjorie's Christmas party might have been the same Christmas the Murphys arrived late for my family's annual drop-in Christmas Eve Party.

For years, our family hosted a Christmas Eve gathering. Friends and neighbors were invited to the house from 7:00 p.m. until 10:00 p.m. on Christmas Eve for holiday small talk, eggnog, hors d'oeuvres, and platefuls of barbeque. There would always be a fire in the fireplace and Christmas music wafting from the stereo. Those Christmas Eve flings required a good deal of preparation, and we Shireys were prepared for our guests except for the year the Murphys caught us off guard.

As I recall that night, the last guests left at about 10:00 p.m. and we quickly put everything away. All the leftover hors d'oeuvres had been emptied into Tupperware bowls and tucked into the fridge. The barbecue was plopped into a bowl of its own and shoved into the back reaches of the freezer. Eggnog was poured back into its container, every last candle was blown out, the fire was down to a few glowing embers, and every Shirey was in some state of undress ready for bed when the doorbell rang and my sister screeched, "It's the Murphys!"

That cry in the night led to mayhem.

My brother was sitting in a recliner by the fireplace with nothing on but his underwear. When he heard the doorbell ring, he grabbed the nearest afghan, wrapped it around his lower half, and dashed for the bedroom.

My mother was in the bathtub. When she heard the bell ring all she could do was say, "Keith! The Murphys are here. The Murphys are here!" to my father who was fast asleep on top of the covers in his green paisley pajamas.

My grandmother heard the cry and dashed from her bedroom to the other bathroom in the hopes of putting her teeth back in. On the way, she passed my grandfather heading in the opposite direction clad only in his plaid boxer shorts and my brother in his afghan.

My sister let the Murphys in after I had a chance to plug the tree back in, light a few candles, and make sure all the half-dressed family members were out of sight.

Mr. and Mrs. Murphy asked, "Are we late?"

"Gosh no," my sister said, "So good of you to drop in. Merry Christmas."

One by one, my brother, mother, father, and grandparents made their way into the living room acting as if everything was fine and dandy. Never mind the fact that Mom's hair was wet and my grandfather's socks didn't match and my grandmother's upper plate wasn't in just right and the hors d'oeuvres were served out of Tupperware bowls.

Try as I may each Advent, I know I won't be fully prepared for Christmas. I will make my list and check it twice and still overlook an item or two. And regardless of what I do this Advent, I know I'll be caught off guard by the One who comes at Christmas. It never fails. He'll come a-calling when my soul is half asleep. The doorbell will ring and I'll rush to light a candle or two and put my house in order.

"Am I late?"

"Gosh no, Lord. So good of you to drop in."

Asleep in the Hay

My Dad was in his element on Christmas Eve for the party, but not as much for the church service.

I'm thinking back to the time he fell asleep during the Christmas Eve service. Dad wasn't normally one to fall asleep at church, mostly because he wasn't one to be at church in the first place. But on Christmas Eve, he'd go. Caught up in the Spirit of the season and relishing what had become a family tradition, he'd go.

He didn't fall asleep at the late service. It's all I can do to stay awake at an eleven o'clock Christmas Eve service. You take someone whose body, mind, and spirit clocks out for the night at nine o'clock and stir in soft, soothing music, a warm, cozy environment, and some flickering candlelight and you've got the makings for dozing off. Dad, who fell asleep on the floor in front of the television by 8:30 p.m. would have been out long before the Call to Worship at 11:00 p.m.

We went to what was billed as the 7:00 Family Service the year Dad dozed off. We sat in a pew mid-way back from the pulpit, Dad sandwiched in between my sister and me in the crowded sanctuary. My attention was focused on the music and carols and pageantry of the night until halfway through the reading of the Christmas story from Luke's gospel I felt a sudden movement to my right. I left the shepherds out in the field keeping watch over their flock by night and turned to see that the tug I felt a moment earlier was my father's head falling forward. There he sat next to me, his chin resting against his neck, sound asleep.

By the time a multitude of the heavenly host was praising God and saying, "Peace on earth, goodwill toward men!" Dad was beginning to make some noise himself. He was wheezing and was well on his way to some full-blown snoring when I patted my brother on his thigh and tapped my sister on her shoulder to call their attention to the situation. They already knew, however, and all my patting and tapping did was set off some belly laughing on all our parts that became more and more uncontrollable. Do you know how it is when you get the giggles in church?

Every time I felt I had myself under control I'd feel my brother's body tremble in the pew next to me or hear my sister struggling to stifle a guffaw, and I'd turn my head just enough to see my Dad sitting there in the pew, hands politely folded on his lap, mouth agape, and off I'd go again.

When the shepherds said to one another, "Let's go over to Bethlehem and see this thing that has happened," Dad's volume was noticeably increasing so I decided to take action. I nudged him with my elbow several times until he grunted once or twice and said something to the effect of, "Wha? Huh? Wha?"

"Wake up," I whispered.

He answered, "I'm meditating," which was all my brother,

sister, and I needed to hear to set us rolling again.

He then fell back asleep. He slept through "Away in a Manger" ("sleep in heavenly peace ..."). He slept through "O Little Town of Bethlehem" ("above thy deep and dreamless sleep the silent stars go by"). Dad slept, we giggled, and I occasionally elbowed him so that he'd come to long enough to grunt, "Meditating."

As I recall, my father awoke at the end of the service when the organist struck the opening chords of "Joy to the World." He awoke and we all stood together and sang. We sang, "Joy to the world, the Lord is come, let earth receive her King."

Christ came long ago and Christ shall come again. When he does, we shall all stand together, the living and the dead, and sing.

A Severe Mercy

My father never made it to Carthage. He would have come down for my ordination, I'm sure, but the month before I knelt on the chancel steps of the church and the congregation laid hands on me, he was diagnosed with cancer that would eventually take his life. He underwent surgery, the first of many to follow, and was recovering at home the weekend of the ordination.

He was not a churchgoer, but he did preach a powerful sermon one Monday Noon about judgment and mercy I have not forgotten.

One snowy January, I had just received my driver's license and was eager to use it. Dad knew as much, but he was quick to point out to me in no uncertain terms that days on which eight inches of snow and ice are on the roads and school is canceled are not days rookie drivers should be on them. He asked me if I understood what he was saying. I said I did.

After he left, I got to thinking it wouldn't hurt anything to go out to Jim Burian's house for the morning. I could drive out there, knock around for a while, and drive home by lunch. I'd be careful. And what Dad didn't know couldn't hurt him, right?

I wrecked the car on the way home. I put on the brakes as I approached an intersection, slid thirty feet or so, and rear-ended the car in front of me. No one was hurt, though I had the distinct impression I was about to be. I called Dad from the nearest pay phone and told him what happened.

Dad asked, "Is everybody all right?" followed by, "I'm on my way."

The right front fender was bent against the tire preventing it from turning. He came and without saying a word used a crowbar to pry the crumpled fender away from the wheel.

He then said, "I'll meet you at home. Drive *straight* home." I nodded and did, anticipating en route how *my* fender was in for a crumpling.

I remember parking the car, getting out, following him into the house, and the door shutting. He then turned to me and in a level, measured voice, asked, "Did I tell you not to drive the car today?"

I nodded yes and winced in anticipation of what was to come.

It didn't. He raised neither his hand nor his voice as he rendered his judgment. "You will order a new fender this afternoon and you will pay for it. You will remove the damaged one, prepare the new one, paint it, and put it on."

I remember lying on my back on the cold concrete floor of our unheated garage on a wintry afternoon, crescent wrench in hand, trying to loosen the bolts holding the bent fender in place. Hands cramped. Knuckles skinned. Nose running.

But this I remember most: his presence through it all. He stood beside me (not over me), and when he saw me struggling without success on the most stubborn, rusted nuts, he laid down next to me, took the crescent wrench in his own strong right hand, and bloodied his own knuckles removing them.

The punishment he meted out to me was this: to allow me to see his disappointment in my ignoring his command, then to stand with me, watch over me, and intercede for me as I strived to right the wrong I had committed against him. And when I could not make right the offense I had committed against him, he stretched his own frame out on the cold concrete and blooded his own knuckles.

Tongue-lashings. Spankings. Banishment to my room. My father's attempts to discipline me sometimes took these forms. But no punishment was as effective or memorable, nor none as redemptive, as the severe mercy I received that cold January forty-some years ago.

Punishment and Penitence

I received rehabilitation at the hands of my father for my transgression, but punishment was meted out to the inmates of the Tennessee State Penitentiary for their sins. Opened in 1898, it now sits empty, forced to close in 1992 due to overcrowding, which a federal judge ruled unconstitutional. "The Green Mile" was filmed there. Many of Nashville's musical elite performed at the prison including Johnny Cash, June Carter Cash, and Loretta Lynn. Music videos were shot there. James Earl Ray, the convicted killer of the Rev. Martin Luther King Jr., was incarcerated there until he died. Over one hundred men were put to death there. Nowadays ghosts are rumored to have taken up residence within.

In response to Jesus' words in Matthew 25, "I was in prison and you visited me," graduates of Vanderbilt Divinity School had begun ministries to the inmates of the prison system and their families. At the invitation of a friend and fellow student, Jennie and I visited an inmate on death row. His photo is tucked into our Carthage scrapbook. Ron and an accomplice were serving life sentences for the rape and murder of a woman whose husband had hired the two to kill her. We visited him regularly and when his wife and children came to town, we took the boys and girl out for the afternoon so their mother could visit their father.

Thirty years later, while visiting our daughter in Missouri over the Fourth of July, Jennie and I celebrated the gift of freedom by going to jail. The Missouri State Penitentiary to be exact, or MSP as Doug, the retired guard, called his former place of employment.

With a free morning before heading on to St. Louis in the afternoon, I googled nearby Jefferson City, the state capital, to look for an interesting place to visit. The top-rated Jeff City attraction according to Trip Advisor is none other than the State Penitentiary.

MSP is closed now. Built in 1836 and closed in 2004, the foreboding grey walls cap a 47-acre bluff overlooking the Missouri River. The first prison west of the Mississippi and for many years the largest, Doug the Jailer told us it held title to the dubious distinction of being the most populated prison in the world when over 5,000 inmates were behind its overcrowded bars. It was also called "America's bloodiest 47 acres" back then, an epithet I understood when I toured the macabre two-century-old cell block and imagined thousands of men convicted of heinous crimes tethered in close quarters to fend for themselves.

We saw the cells that housed gangster Pretty Boy Floyd, Sonny Liston (who learned to fight while imprisoned at MSP and became a heavyweight champion after his release), and James Earl Ray (who escaped from MSP by using his contortionist abilities to fold his body into a bread crate which was then loaded by an accomplice onto a bread truck that carried him to freedom outside the walls. He was on the lam when he assassinated Dr. Martin Luther King, Jr.).

Doug the Jailer told us about "the Auburn System," a philosophy of "rehabilitating" prisoners popular in the 19th century utilizing solitary confinement, flagellation, and other practices whereby conditions were made so brutal that any self-respecting person would vow never to commit another crime that would land him back in such a hellhole again.

Apparently, it didn't work. Not for "Firebug" Johnson anyway. He garnered his nickname by setting a fire that caused $500,000 worth of damage and the deaths of several inmates. Convicted of arson and given an additional 12 years, his repeated violations of prison protocol landed him in one of the musty cells in the basement of the cell block known as The Dungeon where prisoners were caged in solitary confinement in total darkness for 23 hours a day. Doug the Jailer told us Firebug spent a total of 18 years of his sentence in the darkness of The Dungeon. After his release, he wrote a book entitled "Buried Alive for 18 Years in the Missouri Penitentiary."

The tour ended with Doug the Jailer taking us to the Gas Chamber where 40 men received capital punishment for crimes ranging from kidnapping and rape to 1st-degree murder from the mid-1930s to 1989. Embedded in the sidewalk leading to the chamber building was a white cross. We walked over it (or around it) without comment. Just outside the doors of the building was a small plot of ground framed by a one-foot-high white picket fence in which a few flowers were planted.

Why the flowers and decorative fencing? I have no idea. Why the cross? Was it one last prod to repent? I turned the word penitentiary over in my mind as we left that day, free to go where we pleased. It contains the word penitent.

When King David broke about every one of the Ten Commandments in the span of a few days of aberrant, lecherous, murderous behavior midway through 2 Kings (2 Kings 11), what did the Lord God do? Wring him by the neck? Publicly humiliate him? Lock him up with a half dozen other adulterers, liars, and murderers and give him a good taste of "the Auburn System?" Throw him in The Dungeon next to Firebug Johnson?

Nope. That's not what God did. God sent the prophet Nathan to David to try to work repentance—penitence—in David's heart (2 Samuel 12). Psalm 51 is the biblical witness that Nathan's confrontation with David worked. Changed his heart. Rehabilitated him.

Our nation's prison system was begun by—guess who?—Christians. Quakers built prisons back in the late-1700s for the primary purpose of leading convicts to repentance — a change of heart and life. As such, they were called penitentiaries. It was a novel concept at the time and it still is: the belief that God's first impulse toward wayward, sinful human beings is not to inflict punishment but to evoke repentance.

I will never profess to understand the vagaries of the human heart and how to crack the code that cracks our stubborn resistance to admitting wrong and turning to the right. Nor will I ever be able to grasp the mystery of grace that is the Bible's telling us that none other than Jesus Christ was descended from the self-confessed felon David who conspired to murder a woman's husband and was restored to the path of righteousness by his Nathan-motivated repentance.

Moses' Baptism

Just as I had no idea how I was going to officiate at my first funeral until Pastor Ron's righteous rant enlightened me, so it was with my first baptism. I needed some theological mentoring which I received from Brother Hartford of Mt. Zion Baptist Tabernacle.

During one of my chaplaincy rounds at the Nashville hospital, I met a man named Moses. When I first met him he was sitting up in bed thanks to two pillows tucked behind his back. A network of tubes connected to a variety of machines that gurgled, beeped, and buzzed were going to and from his body. Lung cancer. Kidney failure. Respiratory complications. He was not well.

As I was passing by his room one day he called out in his raspy voice, "Hey Chaplain! Come in here for a second. I want to ask you something."

Moses wanted to be baptized.

"Anyone in particular you want to do the baptizing, Moses?"

"Yessir, call Brother Cleveland at the Mt. Zion Baptist Tabernacle."

I did as Moses asked only to find that Brother Cleveland of whom Moses spoke had died twenty years ago.

"Moses, you mean you haven't been to church in over 20 years?

"It's been more'n that, I 'spect."

He then traced the path his life had taken over the past decades. He recounted for me the death of his wife in the fifties – "I mean to tell you, Chaplain, she sure was a fine woman. Yessir, she sure was a fine woman."

There followed a bout with alcoholism, the loss of his job with the railroad, and a series of part-time jobs that gave him enough to survive on, but nothing more.

"Chaplain, I don't guess I cared 'bout much those years. Couldn't have cared if I lived or died. Just didn't care no way."

Sometime later, he gave up the bottle, got a full-time job as a janitor at one of the elementary schools in the city, had several years of sobriety and satisfaction, then retirement, and then cancer. Between sentences he sucked in oxygen from the mask over his face, continuing on until he finished.

I said, "Moses, how about if I call Mt. Zion back and explain the situation to them? Maybe we can work something out with the current preacher."

I called and explained the situation and was told they would be delighted to work something out in response to Moses' desire to be baptized.

The next day I met Brother Hartford from Mt. Zion Baptist Tabernacle in the waiting room at the end of the hall. He was dressed in a handsome three-piece suit. He was accompanied by a man he introduced as Deacon Perkins who was also dressed in suit and tie and a woman he introduced as

Sister 'Lizabeth who wore a dress, high heels, and a Sunday bonnet.

Moses wanted to be baptized but there was a problem. Though the hospital allowed persons to be baptized in the physical therapy tubs downstairs, Moses' doctor said he couldn't be immersed with all his life-sustaining tubes snaking in and out of him. Though Baptist Brother Hartford was amenable to baptizing Moses by pouring water over his head and explaining the doctor's orders, Moses demurred, insisting that he be immersed. In his mind, baptism meant immersion. There was no other way.

I was stymied. To buy some time, I said to Moses, "Would you excuse us for a moment? We'll be right back."

In the hallway outside Moses' room, I turned to my ministry cohorts and asked, "What do you think we should do?" After a long, silent pause, Brother Hartford had an idea. He said, "Follow me."

When our quartet processed into Moses' room his eyes lit up and the faint trace of a smile appeared on his face. Brother Hartford, Deacon Perkins, Sister 'Lizabeth, and I stepped up next to his bedside. Then Bro. Hartford bent over from the waist, took Moses' hand in his, looked him square in the eyes, and said, "Brother Moses, do you believe in Jesus? Do you believe he's your Lord and Savior? Do you love God?"

To each question, Moses answered, "Yessir, I do," eyes fixed on Brother Hartford.

Brother Hartford continued, "Brother Moses, do you trust me?"

"Yessir, I do."

"Do you believe that what I'm 'bout to tell you is God's

truth?"

"Yessir, I do."

Then, with his eyes fixed on Moses, Brother Hartford said, "Brother Moses, you've just been baptized."

Moses made no reply.

Without batting an eyelash and eyes yet fixed on Moses, Bro. Hartford quoted Matthew 3:11 from memory—"One who is more powerful than I is coming after me; I am not worthy to carry his sandals. He will baptize you with the Holy Spirit and with fire."

"Brother Moses," he continued, "you don't need no water baptism. Jesus just baptized you with the Holy Spirit. Brother, I mean to tell you – you just been baptized."

"I have?" Moses asked.

"I mean to tell you, Brother, baptized in the Holy Spirit — the Holy Spirit of the *Living* God!"

With that, I watched as a tear welled up in Moses' left eye, fell over the edge of his eyelid, and tumbled down his cheek. More followed.

Sister 'Lizabeth burst forth with a "Hallelujah!" Deacon Perkins burst forth with an "Amen!" and I let loose with a "Praise God!" of my very own.

Brother Hartford, meanwhile, just kept holding on to Moses' hand and looking into his eyes, never wavering, no not once, and saying over and over again in a tone of resolute assurance, "You been baptized in the Holy Spirit. Yessir, been baptized in the Holy Spirit of the *Living* God."

Moses wept with evident joy, his face transfigured.

For the next few weeks, I spotted Brother Hartford, Deacon Perkins, and Sister 'Lizabeth many times at the hospital on their way to visit with their newest church member. Moses died not long thereafter. He was at peace. Whole. It was in the spring, not too long before Easter.

Bowling for Baptism

I, too, was baptized not long before Easter. It was at Central Christian Church (Disciples of Christ) in Warren, OH, on Palm Sunday, 1972. I wondered how long Rev. Cox was going to hold Barbie Gibbons under the water because I was next. After he raised her up from the water, he extended his hand to me. As I walked down into the baptistery, I heard someone blow their nose in the congregation, and without even looking I knew it was my grandfather, crying. At the age of 64, he knew the importance of my baptism. At the age of 13, I did not. Hence, he cried. I merely fretted over the temperature of the water and how long I'd need to hold my breath.

To prepare us for baptism, Rev. Cox led an eight-week Pastor's Class on Saturday mornings. Candidates for baptism were asked to attend. I did not go to any of them. Why? I bowled on Saturday mornings. A guy has his priorities, right? So, rather than eight weeks of Bible study on the meaning of baptism and church membership, I concentrated on throwing strikes and picking up spares at Echo Lanes.

As it turned out, the sum total of my preparation for baptism consisted of an hour-long visit with Rev. Cox in the dining room of our home. He told my mother he would baptize me with all the other non-bowlers provided I could evidence to him some knowledge of Scripture. In my mind, that meant I would forever be a non-baptized bowler because my knowledge of the Bible was, well, ... minimal.

I crammed for the exam by opening the family Bible to page 1 and reading through to about page 3 before giving up. Rev. Cox came by the house at 7 p.m. in his suit and tie, toting a well-worn Bible. I came down the steps wearing an Oakland Raiders football jersey and carrying a Bible that was well-worn on pages 1, 2, and 3.

The quiz commenced and I got a perfect score. How so?

Rev. Cox's quiz consisted of reeling off a series of biblical names. I was to tell him if they were from the Old or New Testament. I'm sure there was more, but that is what I have retained across the past nearly fifty years. My strategy was as follows: if the name sounded old, I'd say "Old Testament" and if it sounded new, I'd say "New Testament."

It worked like a charm. Ezekiel: Old. Methuselah: Old. *Really* old. Deuteronomy: Old. *Definitely* old. Isaiah: Old. Matthew: New. Luke: New. Paul: New. Mary: New. I got 'em all right. In retrospect, I'm glad he didn't ask me about Samuel or David. I would have guessed wrong.

As it turned out, I passed the test. Rev. Cox told my mother he would be willing to baptize me along with the rest of the Pastor's Class on Palm Sunday. So it was I was baptized along with a dozen or so others after which I received a certificate, a brand new Bible – King James red-letter edition with artificial black leather and a zipper – and a box of offering envelopes.

Thirty-plus years ago, at a General Assembly of our Disciples of Christ, I ran into Rev. Cox. He said he had heard through the grapevine I had been ordained. He congratulated me warmly and, though we didn't speak about it, I remembered that Pastor's Class in our dining room and how I had thought I had pulled one over on the old preacher when in fact he had demonstrated to me what baptism is all about—the unmerited embrace of various and sundry tax collectors, sinners, and Saturday morning bowlers in the arms of grace.

Blind and Deaf

Even as I recall with thanksgiving all the glimpses of grace I have been afforded, I shudder to think of how many things I just plain missed. "Whoever has eyes to see, let them see. Those with ears to hear, let them hear," Jesus said.

Several years ago while on sabbatical, Jennie and I sat next to an elderly couple en route from Glasgow to London. As the woman boarded with her husband's assistance, I noted a badge pinned conspicuously on her lapel. The red block letters read: BLIND AND DEAF.

Their manner of communicating with each other was a thing of beauty to behold. She was able to speak, so would lean toward him and whisper in his ear. After speaking, she would then hold her hand in front of herself at chest level, palm open, thumb up, fingers extended. He would then "speak" to her by extending his index finger and touching various places on her palm and fingertips in a sequence that communicated his response. They communicated effortlessly: her whisper followed by the presentation of her hand followed by the fluid motion of his finger rapidly typing out his response.

Though I couldn't make heads or tails of what they were "saying" to each other, I got the gist of much of their conversation.

In one exchange, she patted him on the shoulder, whispered something into his ear, and then extended her hand as he first checked his watch and then touched her palm with three brief strokes. He told her the time.

On another occasion, she patted his leg gently as she spoke, then extended her hand as he gently signed his response with his finger, concluding the message with an affectionate peck on the cheek. I understood.

I even watched him tell her a joke. He tapped her, she extended her hand, and then he proceeded with a rather lengthy sequence of touches that evoked several accompanying chuckles. When his last three touches led to a loud guffaw on her part, I knew he had just "touched" the punch line. Theirs was a loving communication forged between lifelong partners.

It dawned on me that regarding perceiving God's presence in my life and hearing God's voice, I might as well be tagged BLIND AND DEAF. And yet, just as that couple had learned to speak without the benefit of eye or ear, so does God seek to be in communion with us. Christians across the ages have learned to extend the hand of faith upon which are found the fingers of prayer, Bible study, fellowship, stewardship, and service. God touches us in each of these spiritual disciplines, through them communicating Divine presence and power in ways we can truly see and hear.

To those who do not speak the language of faith, our manner of communicating with God must make no sense whatsoever. I couldn't understand the system of touches and strokes that were exchanged between the man and woman on the bus. But I saw for myself that in their desire to show and express their love, they had overcome the barriers of sight and hearing and truly did communicate.

I came back from that sabbatical more keenly aware of the importance of the spiritual disciplines for our communicating with God who seeks always to communicate with us. I determined anew to continue to give myself to living my life with my hand outstretched fully before me, anticipating God's touch.

Faith tells me that one day the woman and man on the bus will be able to truly see each other's faces and hear each other's words. What joy! And we who now "see in a mirror dimly" when it comes to communicating with our God will also see face-to-face.

The Night with *Night*

It took a Nobel laureate and a dressing down by a friend to remove the scales from my eyes and penetrate my clueless insensitivity.

Holocaust survivor, author, professor, and humanitarian Elie Wiesel died at the age of 87 having authored nearly 60 books. *Night* is a slim one-hundred-page volume that chronicles his remembrance of the Nazi concentration camps of Auschwitz and Buchenwald. His mother and younger sister were killed at Auschwitz. Wiesel and his father were then deported to the concentration camp at Buchenwald where his father died just months before the camp was liberated by the U.S. Third Army on April 11, 1945. *Night* was first published in 1960. It has been reprinted numerous times since then and has sold millions. I was in Divinity School in 1982 when I was assigned to read it. Reading *Night* changed my life. I'm embarrassed to share how.

During my Divinity School years, I lived in the Disciples Divinity House at Vanderbilt, a three-story apartment building with studio and one-bedroom apartments available to Divinity School students at below-market rates.

Life in the Disciples House offered residents a rich community of kindred minds, twenty or so of us who went to class in the daytime, shared an evening meal, spent whatever time was needed post-dinner for homework, and then closed out the day in earnest conversation or frivolous fellowship, often at a nearby pub.

The day we were assigned *Night*, it was the only homework we were given. I ate dinner, scampered off to my room to read, and was delighted to see that the book was a slim one hundred pages. "This'll be a breeze," I remember thinking to myself. "Two hours max and I'm outta here." I'm a fairly fast reader. Wiesel's writing in *Night* is minimalist. There was a lot of white space on those one hundred pages. Bottom line: I read *Night*, took a shower, and was knocking on my buddy Bill's door by 8:30 p.m.

"It's open," he yelled from inside.

I opened the door. He was sitting on his couch holding his copy of *Night* in his hands.

I said, "You're still reading, huh?"

He said, "What do you mean *still* reading?"

"I'm done," I said. "It was easy. Are you almost done? I'm ready to go out."

Bill leaped out of his chair. Clearly angered, he stood up and walked toward me, his copy of the book in his hand. "What do you mean you're done reading?" he barked. "What do you mean 'It was easy?' What the hell do you mean 'Are you ready to go out?'" A vein in his forehead throbbed as he spoke.

He continued. "There is no way you can read this book in two hours! There is no way a thinking, feeling human being can read what is written in these pages about what this man witnessed human beings doing to other human beings, toss the book aside, and go out. No way! Are you kiddin' me?"

Shaking the book at me, his eyes focused on mine, he said, "You haven't read this book. You may have glided your eyes over the words, but let me tell you something: *You. Have. Not. Read. This.* Go back to your room and *read* the book. It will take you the rest of the night … *if* you can get through it at all!"

I did not respond. I walked back to my room to ponder what just hit me.

Bill's admonishment changed forever the way I read. Years later, I read somewhere that "the purpose of Bible study is not to get through the Bible, but for the Bible to get through you." That's what Bill was trying to get through my immature mind the night he excoriated me for my flippant reading of *Night*. I had gotten through one of the most harrowing accounts of the Holocaust ever written in two hours and I was ready to go out on the town? Really?

Clearly, the book had not gotten through me. I was opaque to its significance until my friend sent me back to read it again.

To this day, I read with respect, earnestness, and expectation, especially holy writ: Scripture, great literature, poetry, the work of brilliant essayists, and the musings of gifted journalists.

I'm a better man for being a better reader. It all started that night with *Night*.

An Advent Disposition

Thanks to Bill's tongue-lashing, I developed an Advent disposition. There are Christmas, Easter, and Pentecost personalities – those extroverted, bright-faced, life-of-the-party people without whom the world and church would be a much duller, all-too-serious place. Thank God for such people. But I am not one of them. I am an Advent person. Introverted, introspective, I am an incurable ponderer, prone to sitting for long spells in hushed silence contemplating the why and wherefore of it all.

Eugene Peterson helped me understand how my Advent disposition could inform my ministry. Reflecting on *Ulysses*, James Joyce's epic novel detailing one day in the life of Dublin's Leopold Bloom, he wrote:

> Two-thirds of the way through this meander of narrative, I saw what I could be doing, *should* be doing, in my pastoral work. Before Ulysses, I had never looked at the workday aspects of ministry as particularly creative. I knew they were important, and I accepted them as basic tasks to be carried out whether

I felt like it or not, but, except for occasional epiphanies, I did not find them very interesting ....

And then one day while reading *Ulysses* ... an earthquake opened a fissure at my feet and all my assumptions of ordinariness dropped into it. All those routines of the pastoral vocation suddenly were no longer routines.

Joyce woke me up to the infinity of meaning within the ordinariness of the ordinary person in the ordinary day. Now I knew my work: this is the pastor's work. I wanted to be able to look at each person in my parish with the same imagination and insight and comprehensiveness with which Joyce looked at Leopold Bloom. The storyline is different, for the story that is being worked out right before my eyes, if only I can stay awake long enough to see it, is not the Greek story of Ulysses, but the gospel story of Jesus.

I saw now that I had two sets of stories to get straight. I already knew the gospel story pretty well. But I had another set of stories, these stories of Leopold Bloom and Buck Mulligan, Jack Tyndale, Mary Vaughn, Olaf Odegaard, and Abigail Davidson—I had to get these stories straight, too. The Jesus story was being reworked and re-experienced in each of these people, in this town, in this day. And I was here to see it take shape, listen to the sentences form, observe the actions, discern character and plot. I wanted to see the Jesus story in each person in my congregation with as much local detail and raw experience as James Joyce did with the Ulysses story in

> the person of Leopold Bloom and his Dublin friends and neighbors." (*Under the Unpredictable Plant: An Exploration in Vocational Holiness*, 124-25.)

Though Peterson first published those words in 1992, it wasn't until over a decade later that I read them. Doing so helped explain to me my delight in collecting the stories of Mr. Bill and Billie Ruth, Margaret and Aunt Hazel, Kenneth, Moses, and the Carters, seeing the Christ story in the narrative of people's daily lives, chronicling the Word made flesh dwelling among us wearing BLIND AND DEAF buttons, loosening rusty nuts with bloodied knuckles, and playing a mandolin filled with rattlesnake rattles – this is what I yearned to do, work that suited my Advent disposition.

The season of Advent is contemplative, too. For one month each year Advent defies convention, shies away from the hustle and bustle marking the weeks leading up to Christmas, goes off to a quiet, darkened corner, and ponders. Advent spends the four weeks shrouded in deep purple, a color of depth, a solemn color. The color purple, like the season that wears it, reflects deeply.

But don't get us wrong, Advent and me. Should you catch us off in a corner, silent and pensive with a faraway look in our eyes, don't worry. Nothing's wrong. We're not sad. Neither are we feeling left out. What we're doing is praying. If our praying looks labored, difficult – it is. It is difficult because precisely *what* we want, *who* we want, is not quite clear yet. All we know is our souls' deep longing for some*thing*, some*one*. So we pray, yet for what we know not.

For now, all we can say is two words: O come. Over and

over again, we say the same words: O come. O – a long plaintive sound. A yearning. Come – an asking. A begging.

What Advent and I are praying for in our hushed corner in sighs deeper than words is salvation. And the song Advent and I sing, the carol that captures the brooding, yearning, purple spirit which we feel is this: "O Come, O Come Emmanuel."

And if Advent and I could choose a verse that would give voice to our yearning, it would be this, sung *a cappella*, in a darkened sanctuary, late on a December night: "O come, Desire of nations, bind / All peoples in one heart and mind / Bid envy, strife, and quarrels cease; / Fill the whole world with heaven's peace."

Advent and I sing those words often. And I tell you that sometimes, late at night, in a darkened sanctuary, if we lean in and listen ever closely, we can hear the silence sing, "Rejoice, Rejoice! / Emmanuel shall come to thee, / O Israel!"

The Real Bible

I'm trying to discern my parishioners' stories within *the* story, the grand narrative of God's redeeming work as recorded in the pages of Scripture.

I have the same Bible today that I carried with me to Carthage forty years ago. It's an Oxford Annotated Revised Standard Version I bought at the Indiana University bookstore the fall semester of my sophomore year of college when I took an elective course called "The Bible as Literature." It was taught by a professor in the English Department who was a Shakespeare scholar. He taught the stories of the Bible with such obvious delight and with such passion, reveling in the plot and character development, that I found myself reading the Bible for the first time with eyes provoked to curiosity by his lectures.

Before the acquisition of that Bible, my personal Bible was the artificial black leather-bound King James Version with a zipper that I received from my home church on the day of my baptism. Unread and virtually unopened, its Elizabethan English was a more than adequate barrier to my less-than-motivated desire to read and understand it, so it was relegated to a dusty shelf on a bookshelf for my teen years.

By contrast, the RSV that invited my first foray into the pages of scripture has been rebound and though newer translations have emerged over the years I cannot part with the version that over time has become the repository of innumerable pencil jottings, yellow-highlighted verses, bookmarks commemorating various occasions, even a few obituaries and photographs. Its margins have become a scrapbook for my journey of faith.

Carthage Christian Church had a pulpit Bible. Weighing as much as a barbell, it sat in sentinel witness beside the pulpit. Though I never read from its pages on Sunday – King James, no leather, no zipper—I found a measure of encouragement and authority having it in such close proximity as if somehow its presence next to me lent my youth and inexperience some much-needed reinforcement.

I needed all the help I could get. I showed up on my first Sunday with a full manuscript from which I read each line verbatim. There was no raised ledge on the tilted portion of the Carthage pulpit to hold a manuscript in place so it was only a matter of time (usually just past the introduction) before the slight wisp of wind caused by a hand gesture would send sermon pages fluttering off the pulpit to the chancel carpet beneath. I accused the congregation of waxing the pulpit to increase the chances of a runaway manuscript, their hijinks motivated by their desire that their preachers-in-training not be tied to manuscripts at all but rather be able to communicate a sermon to them with both hands free and both eyes making contact. In a few short weeks, I gave up on reading from the manuscript and though to this day I have a full manuscript before me, I rarely turn to it.

As for my reading from my RSV over the esteemed King James, nobody ever said anything except for one occasion at a funeral in Carthage. As I read aloud "In my Father's house are many rooms," a man sitting near the front who expected to hear King James' "mansions" when I said "rooms" said disdainfully in a whisper that could be heard throughout the sanctuary, "He's readin' from that *new* Bible!"

I guess if it were my choice between a mansion or a mere room for eternity, I'd want the mansion, too.

During one of my chaplaincy visits back in Nashville at the hospital, I was paged by the nursing staff (not in the middle of the night this time) and referred to a particular room. Upon introducing myself, the woman asked me "if I would read her some Bible." When I obliged, she pointed to a stack of Bibles a half-dozen high on her bedside tray and said, "Take your pick."

She said, "I brought 'em all with me. I've got the New English Bible, the Reader's Digest Bible, the Living Bible, the Jerusalem Bible, the Revised Standard Version and, of course," she added matter-of-factly, "I've got the real Bible right there, too."

"The real Bible?" I asked.

"Right there on top," she said and pointed to a tattered King James Version, black leather bound, HOLY BIBLE emblazoned on the cover in gold-embossed letters, red-letter edition (no zipper, though).

I smiled and told her that I had a real Bible, too, and told her the story of how it was presented to me on the day of my baptism in 1972. I told her of the Living Bible that ended up in my hands while in high school that was so much easier for me to understand and the Revised Standard Version I bought before my first religion class and the pocket-sized New Testament with an aqua cover that my wife had received years ago for memorizing Bible passages in Bible School but that I, through avarice and stealth, slid into my possession. (If she memorized it, why did she need it anyway?). I told her I also had the Bible my Dad was given when he was baptized (Unread. I found it in the attic at home, spine still in pristine condition) as well as the Bible my brother was given when he was baptized (It was not far from where I found Dad's and in the same mint condition).

I smiled and said, "I bet my pile of Bibles is higher than yours."

She grinned. "But I've got more at home!"

"Okay," I said, "you win. Which one do you want me to read from and what do you want me to read?"

"Oh, why not read from the real one," she said. "Some Psalms would be really nice."

You, too, may have your own collection of Bibles, each with its own story, each marking a different stage in your life's journey, some purchased, some received as a gift, some treasured hand-me-downs. And I suspect that you have your favorite among them, your own *real* Bible that has your indelible markings on its pages and in its margins.

Ultimately, of course, we need to translate the text into our own lives and allow "the Word to become flesh and dwell among us full of grace and truth." I think that's the Revised Standard Version, but having neither my stack of Bibles nor manuscript before me, I'm not absolutely sure.

Bible a la Carte

I do know this about the real Bible: it was a labor of love to produce. At Carthage, our Bible Study/Coffee Fellowship Hour took place around the kitchen table that occupied the room directly behind the pulpit side of the chancel, the same room that had the church's sole bathroom adjoining it.

The table sat six comfortably, eight at capacity, which is about the range of numbers we would have on any given Sunday for the hour before worship. There was no curriculum. Most Sundays we discussed the Scripture on which I was going to preach that Sunday. Having researched and deliberated on the text during the week in Nashville, I was prepared to lead a free-flowing discussion with the knights of the Carthage kitchen roundtable on Sunday morning.

One Sunday I detoured from the text of the day for a topical study I dubbed "How the Bible Came to Be." I had learned in one of my classes at Divinity School the fascinating account of the Bible's long journey from word-of-mouth stories among the tribes of ancient Israel to our modern English translations.

One particular piece of the story that I shared with the

Carthage Coffee Klatch and that captured my imagination is related in William Barclay's *Introducing the Bible*. Before the days of copying machines and the printing press, the Bible was copied by hand. Given the size of the Scriptures – my RSV from IU days is 1,514 pages from Genesis 1 through Revelation 22 – I asked the folks if they could imagine the amount of time spent in producing a single copy of the Old and New Testaments. Taking it one step further I asked, 'Given such a labor-intensive venture, how much do you think the finished product would cost?'

Barclay's book suggested an answer. In the sixth century, persons who copied manuscripts received twenty to twenty-five denarii per hundred stichoi. Given that a denarius was about ten cents and a stichos was about sixteen syllables, that means that it cost about two dollars to copy one hundred lines of the Bible. As Barclay figured it, that would mean that the Gospel of Matthew itself, apart from the cost of the paper on which it was printed, would cost about fifty dollars.

All of which got me thinking and calculating. If Matthew cost $50 and there are 28 chapters in Matthew, then dividing 50 by 28 tells me that it cost roughly $1.75 per chapter. I then went through and made a note of how many chapters there are in each book of the Old and New Testaments, added those numbers together, and came up with a total of 1,189 chapters in the Bible. Multiplying 1,189 chapters by my previously calculated copyist's rate of $1.75 per chapter gave me a final figure of $2,080 for a copy of the entire Bible. The price tag on a single copy of the Bible in the sixth century was over $2,000.

I said to Harry Murduck and Mr. Bill, Billie Ruth, Polly,

Kenneth, and Frances Sue, I can't help but wonder how many of us would own a Bible at that price. Would you pay $2,000 for a Bible? If you did, would the fact that you paid so much for it make it any more precious?

Would you regard it any differently if it cost you more to obtain?

I continued. Let's say I'm on a fixed income and can't afford the $2,000 Bible. Since the copyist will provide me with any portion of the Scriptures I want at the cost of $1.75 per chapter, it would be possible for me to buy the Bible in a piecemeal fashion. So, if I could buy only the chapters and/or entire books that my limited budget would allow, for what parts of the Bible would I pay $1.75 a chapter?

Without a whole lot of thought on my part, I told them what my order would be. Though I'd order from both Testaments, for the sake of time I only named my New Testament order:

Matthew 1 and 2 for his account of the Christmas story, 5-7 for the Sermon on the Mount, and 25 and 26 for the sheep and the goats and the Last Supper. 7 chapters @ $1.75 = $12.25.

All of Luke (I'm partial to Luke's account of Jesus) and all of John (John's account of Christ is literally "out of this world"). 45 chapters @ $1.75 = $78.75.

Acts 1, 2, 9, and 10 for Pentecost, Paul's conversion, and Peter's encounter with Cornelius. 4 chapters @ $1.75 = $7.00.

All of Romans. No substitute for Paul's masterful explication of what we believe as Christians. 16 chapters @ $1.75 = $28.00.

1 Corinthians 12, 13, 15 for Paul's inspired writings about

the church, life in the Spirit, love, and the resurrection. 3 chapters @ $1.75 = $5.25.

2 Corinthians 4 and 5 for some of the absolute gems of the New Testament. 2 chapters @ $1.75 = $3.50.

Ephesians 1 and 2 for "God's plan for the fullness of time" and all 4 chapters of Philippians for Paul at his best. 6 chapters @ $1.75 = $10.50.

2 Timothy 4 for "I have fought the good fight … ," Philemon for the persuasiveness and brilliance of Paul's littlest letter, Hebrews 11 and 12 for the roll call of faith, and 1 Peter 2 for its description of our high calling. 5 chapters @ $1.75 = $8.75.

Revelation 3, 19, 21, 22 for the letters to the churches, "I stand at the door and knock," the Hallelujah Chorus, and "a new heaven and new earth." 4 chapters @ $1.75 = $7.00.

Total bill = $161.00.

I then turned the floor (and the table) over to them. What would they order? How much would their Bible cost?

They leafed through their Bibles in search of cherished chapters. Harry excused himself a few times to use the adjoining room. Billie Ruth replenished Mr. Bill's decaf. Kenneth said he'd certainly have to order his own Hebrews chapter twelve seeing that it mentions running with perseverance the race that is before us. Polly, like the lady with the real Bible in Nashville, preferred certain Psalms. Mr. Bill and Frances Sue chimed in with their own "can't do withouts."

We carried on until Chet cracked the door open, smiled, pointed to his wristwatch, and said, "Time for worship."

As they walked out of the room into the sanctuary, I watched as Mr. Bill passed by the pulpit. He reached out with his right hand and touched the big Bible, just sort of patted it appreciatively on his way to his pew.

Aunt Gertrude's Bookshelf

Psalm 90:10 says, "The days of our life are seventy years, or perhaps eighty if we are strong." Many of Carthage Christian's members either did not receive the Psalmist's memo about the length of life – 70 years; 80 if you're lucky – or else they received the Psalmist's foray into gerontology but set it aside and barreled on through the seventh, eighth, and ninth decades of their lives with an unremitting verve that is a wonder to behold.

Throughout my ministry, the name of one of the church's senior members would come up and upon hearing their name, a unison chorus of adoration would arise around the office. Rarely would a day go by when I didn't overhear someone say upon hanging up the telephone after a conversation with one of the matriarchs or patriarchs, "That was So-and-So. Don't you just love him? Isn't she a peach? God love her! Hearing from him makes my day."

The evocation of such affectionate accolades reminds me of the Psalmist lauding seniors whose lives have accrued a wise, resilient righteousness that blesses upcoming generations:

The righteous flourish like the palm tree,
and grow like a cedar in Lebanon.
They are planted in the house of the Lord;
they flourish in the courts of our God.
In old age they still produce fruit;
they are always green and full of sap,
showing that the Lord is upright. (Psalm 92:12-15)

Jennie had two aunts that lived to be one hundred. I remember visiting her Aunt Gertrude, then 104 years old. She lived in Harrisonburg, VA, in the heart of the Shenandoah Valley, where she was born in the 1890s, the third of eight daughters of a Presbyterian minister. I don't know exactly when Aunt Gertrude was baptized. Sometime before WWI, no doubt, but whenever it was, it took. She was a disciple of Jesus Christ in the fullest sense of the word. Having apprenticed herself to Jesus, she spent a lifetime learning the Master's ways and my, did it show.

On the desk behind where she sat when we visited, I saw the ever-present pile of books—a testament to her lifelong delight in the word (and Word). I saw a hymnal, a devotional book, her Bible, and an eclectic smattering of who-knows-what-else including a book entitled *Soul Tsunami* by Leonard Sweet. Sweet is a church futurist, a guy who writes stuff that is way out there in terms of what the Church may be like several decades from now.

So what was a 104-year-old doing reading such stuff? She knew she wouldn't be around several decades down the road to see if any of what Sweet wrote is right or not. So I asked her why. "Oh," she said, "He keeps me awake. And I'm interested in the future of the church." This she said with a glint in her eye and a voice that connoted hope and enthusiasm.

I hope that when I'm 104 I'll be filled with hope and enthusiasm for the future of the church. Like Aunt Gertrude. Like so many of the wise, winsome elders at Carthage and the other churches I've served, the mere mention of whose names evoke sweet sighs of affection and gratitude.

I want to be like them when I grow up.

Mrs. Beagle's Birthday Zinnias

In a parable of some note, Jesus tells of a sower who went out to sow. Remember the plot? The fella scatters seed by the bushel in all sorts of terrain – some end up in a briar patch, some end up in a veritable rock quarry, and some find their way into a thicket full of weeds. In short, the seed gets sown in every sort of nook and cranny that doesn't promise a good yield come harvest time. We read the parable and shake our heads disparagingly at this guy who sows seed with reckless abandon in sorry-looking soil.

One summer during my undergraduate years, job prospects for college students were mighty bleak. In an act of desperation, I took out an ad in the local paper that read something like: College student wants to mow lawns. Very reasonable. (The ad was a polite way of saying: College student will do just about anything for bucks.)

Well, the ad worked. My lime green Lawn Boy mower covered a lot of turf between May and September, enough anyway to send me back to school for another year.

One of my customers was a woman by the name of Mrs. Beagle. She stood about 4'7" in high heels and I was 6'4" barefoot, so it must have been a curious sight on that first day I met her when she took my arm and led me on a guided tour of her "yard." I say "yard" tentatively because Mrs. Beagle's "yard" was not a yard but rather bore a striking resemblance to an Amazon rainforest. I had never seen such an impressive variety of weeds in all of my days. I was certain that if I ventured off her sidewalk more than a few steps I'd stand a chance of stumbling across a lost civilization of some sort.

Mrs. Beagle struck up a deal with me then and there. In short, she told me how she was older than the hills and didn't figure to be around next summer and the one thing she wanted to be done before she died was to have her "yard" in good shape and her "flower bed" weeded out. Though I couldn't see either a yard or a flower bed, I took up the challenge. Armed with a sickle and garbage bags I set to hacking away, supervised all the while by my diminutive employer.

As the summer progressed, things began to take shape at the Beagle estate. In fact, I took quite a liking to her. One day early on, after I had managed to clear a spot, she shuffled out to where I was on all fours and handed me a package.

"Plant 'em!" she barked.

"Where?" I asked.

"Right there in the flower bed you just cleared off," was the reply.

As it turned out, Mrs. Beagle had a whole slew of kinfolk scattered all across the country, none of whom lived nearby, nearly all of whom had forgotten about their eccentric aged matriarch, but one of whom had sent her a single packet of zinnia seeds on her birthday. And that's all she got on her birthday – a single packet of zinnia seeds which she was now telling me to plant in her rediscovered flower bed.

"Tell you what," I said, "Why don't you plant 'em? They're your birthday present."

I handed the zinnia seeds back to her.

She bit off the corner of the packet, dumped the contents into the palm of her wrinkled hand, and, with all the energy she could muster, heaved the whole slew of seeds in the general direction of the flower bed.

"There," she huffed, "Now water 'em."

Then she shuffled back inside.

To make a long story short, come late August Mrs. Beagle's yard was a yard again. The fearsome Amazon weed forest was brought to its knees by my trusty sickle, and the lime-green Lawn Boy took care of the rest. As for the flower bed ... well, the darndest thing came to pass. Mrs. Beagle ended up with the most glorious batch of zinnias you've ever laid eyes on. A whole multitude of Beagle's Birthday zinnias in every color of the rainbow popped up in that flower bed. In fact, when Mrs. Beagle led me out to the plot of ground and I laid eyes on those zinnias, I was absolutely dumbfounded.

"See," she beamed, "I told ya they'd grow!"

Though I know better, I could have sworn that Mrs. Beagle stood six foot tall that day as she and I took in the sight of those magnificent zinnias.

She died later that fall.

Sometimes I would look at the red brick building a block north of the Smith County Courthouse, consider its demographics (average age 70), average worship attendance (15), and average tenure of pastorates (two years), and shake my head at the prospects for fruitful ministry. It didn't seem like fertile soil, not to mention the youthful inexperience of the farmer. But whenever I doubted the possibilities for fruitful ministry, I envisioned the Holy Spirit in the form of a feisty 4' 7" matriarch coming alongside me, biting off the corner of a packet of gospel seed, heaving them all toward the front door of Carthage Christian Church, and saying, "There! Now water 'em."

For nearly three years, I did.

A Righteous Man

At just under three years, my tenure as minister of Carthage Christian Church was the longest in twenty-five years. Fifteen pastors served the church from 1956-1982, with an average tenure of fewer than two years. The pattern was for a second-year student at Vanderbilt Divinity School to serve the church in their second and third years of the three-year M.Div. program, then pass the baton of leadership at graduation to another second-year student. Often, however, the church had to settle for a one-year ministry.

The man who served the church the longest, from 1948-1956, was Herman A. Norton. Dr. Norton left Carthage to join the Vanderbilt faculty as a professor of American Church History and Dean of the Disciples Divinity House, the three-story apartment building a few blocks from the Divinity School where I lived from 1981-1985. For nearly four decades until he died in 1992, Dr. Norton was a one-man encourager of Vanderbilt Disciples students. He raised money for scholarships, taught Disciples history classes, recruited new students, oversaw the upkeep and maintenance of the apartment building, and provided references for Disciples students seeking their first churches after graduation – an indefatigable advocate, friend, and pastor to decades of aspiring ministers. In addition to the above, he attained the rank of Brigadier General while serving in the U.S. Army Reserves, having served in the Army Chaplaincy in the Pacific Theater during WWII.

"Herman stories," as we affectionately called them, were the stuff of legend. An expert on modern religious cults, the story was told of Dr. Norton's research of snake handlers and their churches. The way I heard it, Dr. Norton established contact with a member of a church who agreed to meet him at a gas station somewhere in the nether regions of eastern Tennessee. His guide would then take him to the church service where he could be a firsthand witness to the goings-on. When the weekend of the date was at hand, Herman received a call from the son of his contact informing him that his father had been bitten by a snake the previous weekend and died. Herman expressed his sympathy to the young man and, angling for another invitation to attend the services, asked him, "Are you a member of the congregation?" To which the man responded, "Hell no! I ain't crazy."

Herman's lectures on American church history, especially his classes dedicated to the Second Great Awakening and the renowned Cane Ridge Revival of 1801, was must-see TV. As Dr. Walter Harrelson, a longtime colleague on the faculty put it, "His lectures were never long. But he was so skilled literarily and rhetorically, that he was always a popular lecturer." To illustrate the manifestations of Pentecostal fervor that broke out during the revival, Herman would raise his arms, wave his hands, and dance across the front of the classroom like an ecstatic concertgoer in a mosh pit. The showstopper came when Herman acted out what was referred to as "the barking exercises." Dropping to all fours, his tie dangling downward, he crawled on his hands and knees to the base of an imaginary tree at which he would commence howling at the top of his lungs, treeing the devil. With the windows and door of the classroom open, the reactions of innocent passersby inside and out to the sight and sounds emanating from within evoked riotous laughter.

But I digress. Dr. Norton shaped the lives and ministry of a generation of Disciples pastors – darn good ones at that – and was adored and respected by us all. With our ministry at Carthage in common, I was blessed with a particularly close relationship with him. He often asked me about the members of the congregation and when ninety-year-old Bill Jellicorse died six months after Miz Ella Robinson, I asked Dr. Norton if he would like to serve alongside me at Bill's graveside service. He agreed, but only if I'd drive and let him treat me to lunch at a new restaurant in which he had bought stock called Cracker Barrel. For the hour's drive out and back, he regaled me with tales of his years at the church with his inimitable warmth, wisdom, and humor.

There was no other choice for who would preach my ordination sermon. For the Scripture, Dr. Norton chose the story of Noah's ark. Slipping into the thick accent of his Tidewater Virginia heritage that turned common words into multisyllabic wonders, he began the sermon with the words, "Noah (pronounced Know-er) was a righteous man." He then explicated three aspects of Know-er's righteousness and called me to aspire to the same. I learned from others at whose ordinations Herman preached that they, too, were ordained to the tune of the Know-er sermon which closed with Dr. Norton inviting the ordinand to come forward to kneel on the chancel steps and receive the laying on of hands. Dr. Norton's and Mr. Bill's hands were the first to be placed on me.

Two years later, I invited Dr. Norton to come to the church I was serving in St. Louis. He and his wife Alma, a Carthage native, spent a weekend with us. Dr. Norton taught a class on Disciples History that included a toned-down version of the barking exercise and preached the morning sermon. I do not recall if Know-er was featured or not.

That was the last time I saw Dr. Norton. A few years after, in the summer of 1992, I received a letter from Dr. Rick Harrison, Herman's successor as Dean of the Disciples House:

Dear Friends,

It is my sad duty to report to you the death of Dean Emeritus Herman Norton. Dr. Norton influenced and shaped the lives of many of us who now serve in a variety of forms of ministry. His work with congregations, especially in Virginia, Western Kentucky, and Tennessee, is remembered with appreciation and affection. Let us thank God for the gift to us of the life of Herman Norton.

Last month, I noticed the signatures on my ordination certificate had faded. Many were almost illegible. Most of the signatories are gone, including Dr. Norton. Jennie took the certificate off the wall, removed it from its frame, carefully retraced the signatures with a fine-line pen, and returned it to its place above my desk.

Herman Norton was a righteous man.

It Don't Get Any Better Than This

I received word in the fall of 1997 that the congregation had decided to close. Mr. Bill and Billie Ruth had died. So had Miss Margaret, Aunt Hazel, Polly, and Chet. Harry and Ova were no longer making their seasonal trek to Tennessee. The congregation was down to single digits. It was time.

The last worship service was held on Sunday, October 22. A fellowship supper followed.

I sent a letter to the few remaining members of the congregation on the day before Thanksgiving and read it aloud during our Thanksgiving Eve service at the North Carolina church I was serving. It read:

> All of you have been in my prayers since I received word of Carthage Christian Church's final worship service. It was in Carthage Christian Church that I heard most clearly God's call to ordained ministry. You surrounded my fledgling efforts at preaching and pastoring with patience. You affirmed and encouraged the raw gifts for ministry which I possessed while at the same time, you challenged me to apply

my heart, mind, soul, and might to develop those gifts to their full potential for Christ's service. Best of all, I learned from my years with you that when the local church is at its best, there is nothing like the life which is ours as brothers and sisters in Christ.

I remember my last Easter with you. After the service, we moved the pews out of the way and set up the folding tables. We uncovered the pots and stuck the serving spoons in the casserole dishes. The plastic cups were filled with ice and sweet tea and the sugar and creamer were set out next to the coffee pot. After a blessing, we made our way through the serving line and took our seats in the sanctuary turned fellowship hall.

I sat at a table next to Mr. Bill that day. He approached gingerly, carefully balancing a Styrofoam plate groaning under the weight of ham and turkey, Polly's chicken and dumplings, green beans, new potatoes, sweet potato casserole, corn cakes, and biscuits. That whole mountain of food was capped off with a chicken breast the size of my hand. Upon arriving at his place at the head of the table, he carefully sat his mound of delectables down, took his seat, and tucked a paper napkin in his collar under his chin.

He then paused and looked up with a mischievous grin on his face. Without saying a word he reached out, put his hand on mine, and with the other hand outstretched, he made a panoramic sweep of the entire church.

As I followed with my eyes, his hand swept past

the pulpit and the open doorway in which I could see the kitchen table that had hosted our pre-worship Bible study now laden with food. His hand continued past the communion table at which I had stood for nearly 150 services with him or Kenneth or John eldering at my side, past the other door from which people were emerging with their heaping plates, past the piano from which Margaret had led worship for a half-century before deferring to Jennie, along the south wall of the sanctuary, the east entrance where the front doors opened onto Main Street, and finally the north wall, completing his grand sweep of sacred space.

Having completed his silent panorama, he grinned broadly and said in his rich Tennessee baritone drawl, "David Shirey, it don't get any better than this!"

Mr. Bill was so right.

Grace and Peace to you all,

David Shirey
Pastor, Carthage Christian Church 1982-1985

Phoenix Rising

In June 2002, Jennie and I pulled up in front of the red brick church on Main Street in Carthage for the first time in seventeen years with our three children in tow. It looked the same. As I stood in front of those familiar doors, I remembered the hundred-some Sundays I had arrived and opened them to the sound of Mr. Bill's welcoming voice saying from within, "David Shirey, come into this house!"

Not that day. The front doors were locked. Above them was a placard that read Main Street Church of Christ. Mr. Bill had died years earlier as had Billie Ruth. So had Margaret Westmoreland and Aunt Hazel, John Collette and Polly Alcorn, Chet and Edna Paris, and the Murducks.

The last worship service of Carthage Christian Church was held on October 22, 1995. Shortly after that the building was sold to a Church of Christ congregation and the modest proceeds realized from the sale were used to endow a college scholarship for a deserving Smith County student.

I stepped up to the windows flanking the front doors, cupped my hands to my face, and peered into the narthex where Jennie and I had conducted Sunday school for Travis,

Lyle, and Amanda. I then walked around the corner of the building to the alley where I could peer into the sanctuary. My eyes retraced the path Mr. Bill's hand had led me on that Easter Sunday years before. The pulpit, communion table, and pews were still there. Only the piano and organ were gone, removed by the *a cappella* owners.

I hoisted our youngest daughter, 9-year-old Laura, high enough to where she could see in as her older sister and brother shuffled their feet with patient disinterest.

"C'mon," I said as I put Laura down. "We're going to make a visit."

Kenneth and Frances Sue Robinson were among the last living members of the church. After it closed, they joined the Methodist Church down the street. Though we heard Frances Sue had been diagnosed with Alzheimer's, she recognized Jennie and me, greeted our kids warmly, and smiled as Kenneth, Jennie, and I reminisced.

The hearth above their fireplace was laden with the ribbons, trophies, medals, and certificates 79-year-old Kenneth had accumulated in the ongoing running exploits that had earned him multiple trips to the Boston Marathon and the twenty-five other marathons he had completed after the heart attack he suffered in his mid-fifties. The obituary that was published in *The Tennessean* after his death read, "His most cherished hobby was running/walking while accumulating more than 60,000 miles from the year 1977 until his morning walk the day of his death."

"Kenneth," I told him, "that Turkey Trot you talked me into running in Nashville back in '87 about killed me!" To which he laughed and mentioned some marathon in Georgia he wanted to run in celebration of his upcoming 80th birthday.

I then told them why we'd come back to Carthage. How two months earlier Jennie and I had accepted a call to plant a new church from scratch northeast of Phoenix. How neither of us knew what we were getting ourselves into, how we sensed it was God's doing, though, and how we felt it was important to return to the roots of our call in Carthage to ask for their blessing on our way. I wanted the hands that had been laid on me at my ordination to bless me on my way again.

"Well if anybody can do it," Kenneth said, "I know you two can." To which Frances Sue nodded her head, grinned broadly, and said, "David and Jennie, you know we love you two and we always will."

We prayed, hugged, and walked together out to the car. Kenneth and Frances Sue stood in their driveway as we pulled away, waving a benediction to us as we returned to Main Street and passed the red brick building one last time on the way out of town before turning west.

One year into our ministry in Phoenix, I sent out a hundred or so letters to Jennie and my extended family across the country as well as to members of the congregations we had served in our first twenty years of ministry. In the letters, I shared how we had accepted the call to plant a new church a long way from anywhere we had ever called home, had been in Phoenix for months pounding the pavement and joining every organization we could find in the effort to meet people, and were asking for their prayers and an offering – seed money with which to plant a church amidst desert sagebrush and saguaro cactus.

We mailed out dozens of letters to Missouri, North Carolina, and Indiana. We sent but one letter to Carthage. Kenneth and Frances Sue were the only ones left.

Hardly a week later, I opened our post office box and was surprised to see that an envelope had already been returned. I pulled it out and saw the postmark: Carthage, TN.

Kenneth and Frances Sue are both gone now. So is the red brick building on Main Street in which our lives were joined thirty years ago. But after nine years of ministry in the Arizona desert, Coolwater Christian Church (Disciples of Christ) now serves out of our long-awaited new building.

From the day Kenneth mailed me the manila envelope with the newspaper clippings detailing the fire that destroyed Carthage Christian Church in 2004, I began gathering the stories of what transpired there for a brief season of ministry. Sometimes months would pass before I could complete a story or discern a connection from one episode to the next. More than once, I set the project aside. Finally, the week after Coolwater's first building was dedicated in June of 2011, everything came together, and I was able to complete the manuscript. That same week I learned of Kenneth's death in Carthage at the age of 88 a month before our first worship service in the building for which his and Frances Sue's check served as the first tangible sign of support.

"What's it mean," I asked Jennie, "that Coolwater had to be built and dedicated before the story of Carthage could be completed?"

It was a rhetorical question, of course. Out of the ashes, the phoenix rises.

On the Sunday we dedicated our new building, I came out of the kitchen with a heaping plate of home-cooked fixins', a palm-sized chicken breast atop the whole pile. After sitting down in that sanctuary turned fellowship hall, I paused before eating to pan the whole scene — pulpit, communion table, keyboard, and of course, the people.

They were all there at the tables with us. Through the eyes of faith, I could see them. Mr. Bill and Billie Ruth. Marjorie (Wine, anyone?). Kenneth and Frances Sue. Harry and Ova (The restrooms are to the rear and to the left). Chet with his mandolin. Mr. Robertson and Moses, too. Miz Ella. Mrs. Beagle provided the zinnias for the centerpieces at each table.

"People will come from east and west and north and south, and will take their places at the feast in the kingdom of God" is the way Luke put it (Luke 13:29). Those who have eyes to see are sometimes blessed to catch a glimpse of the promise foreshadowed. When we do, we tuck a napkin into our collars, put pen to paper, and detail as best we can the grace we have seen, muttering in glad adoration, "It don't get any better than this."

Made in the USA
Columbia, SC
03 July 2025

60313782R00086